Jesus says in Matthew 19:14, "Let the little children come to me . . . for the kingdom of heaven belongs to such as these" (NIV). This book does just that. With easy-to-understand examples, illustrations, and exercises, this book simplifies what we grown-ups can tend to overcomplicate in establishing someone in their walk with Jesus. I can envision using these lessons not only with my own children but also with the local college students that my husband and I minister to. This is an excellent resource for helping anyone at any age deepen and strengthen their relationship with God.

ALICE MATAGORA, author of *How to Save the World*

In a fast-paced life, it's sometimes hard to incorporate discipleship and faith fundamentals for our kids on a daily level. *Discipleship for Kids* is a fantastic tool for teaching our younger generation how to engage with Scripture, cultivate a prayer life, and so much more!

TERESA SWANSTROM ANDERSON, author of the Get Wisdom Bible Studies series

Helping Children Grow in Christ

DISCIPLESHIP FOR KIDS

Rebecca Ruybalid Stone

A NavPress resource published in alliance
with Tyndale House Publishers

NavPress

NavPress is the publishing ministry of The Navigators, an international Christian organization and leader in personal spiritual development. NavPress is committed to helping people grow spiritually and enjoy lives of meaning and hope through personal and group resources that are biblically rooted, culturally relevant, and highly practical.

For more information, visit NavPress.com.

For my children.

Contents

For the Grown-Ups

I'll never forget the first time I made nachos for my young daughter. When I set the food in front of her, she stared at the plate for a moment. Then she hovered both of her hands over the mountain of chips and cheese.

Finally, she looked at me and said, "Okay. Okay. How do I do this?"

She didn't know how to dig into what looked like a mess. She didn't even know where to start.

I think about this story each time I encounter people who want to teach children more about God. They're eager to pass on the deeper things of faith but are reluctant because they don't know where to start. Many parents, grandparents, and other caring adults want to be the ones to help the children in their lives discover the Christian life. But the task feels daunting and overwhelming.

Okay. Okay. How do I do this?

First, let me say to you that you can do this. There isn't one right technique. You don't need to have all the Bible knowledge in the world. It's okay if you are learning along with your child, bit by bit. Bite by bite.

This book you are holding is designed for children to read alone or with an adult. Whatever route you choose, please be assured that reading this book is not a race.

You are free. Your children are free. You are not held to an impossible standard of getting through this book in record time. If you need to spend more time than you thought on each chapter, do that. If you find your child is grasping everything in one section but not another, it's okay to slow down.

More importantly, this book is not supposed to be about simply gaining information so you can get things just right for God. *Obeying Jesus? Check! Prayer? Mastered that! Fellowship? Do that every week!* Discipleship is never about perfecting the Christian life. It's about moving forward with Jesus at the center of our lives.

May our Savior be the one to guide you from this day forward. May you learn to trust and obey him always. He is waiting for you to begin. And he will show you how.

Rebecca Ruybalid Stone

Introduction

Think about your life.

What did you think of first? Did you think about part of your body, like your lungs, which help you breathe? Did you think about where you live and go to school? Did you think about the people you see every day?

All these things are important parts of your life. These things are important to God, too.

If you have chosen to follow Jesus, that means you are a Christian. After you accept Jesus as the only one who can save you from sin, you get to live your life with him every day![1]

You can understand more about life with Jesus by looking at the picture of the Wheel on the next page.

The center of a wheel gives it power and makes it go forward. In the Christian life, Jesus is the center. He gives us the strength to live every part of our lives for him.

Prayer is talking to God and listening to him. **The Word** is the Bible, which is an important way God talks to us. **Fellowship** is spending time with other people who love God. **Witnessing** is using our words and lives to let people know that God loves them and wants them to have new life in him.

Each of these spokes on the Wheel connects us to Jesus at the center, who keeps us moving forward in the Christian life. When we spend time talking with God and listening to him, being with people who love God, and letting others know that God loves them, that's obedience in action.

In this book we're going to look at each part of the Wheel so that we know what it's like to live life with God. Let's get started!

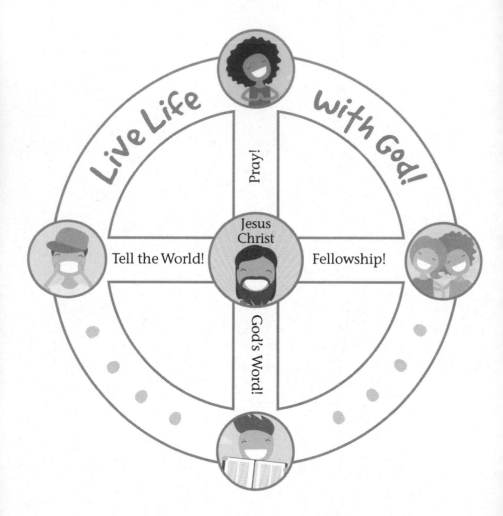

Section 1
Jesus at the Center!

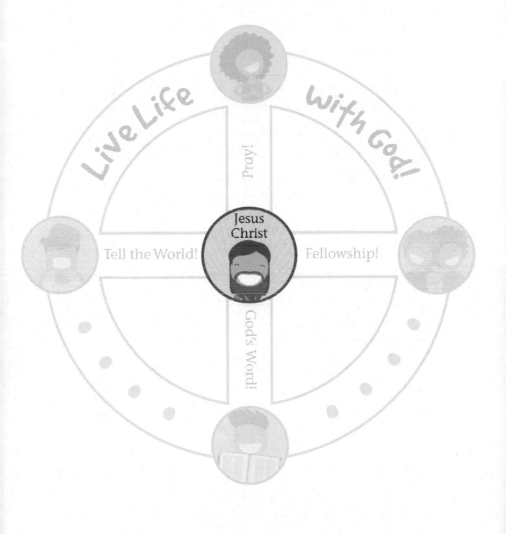

Anyone united with the Messiah gets a fresh start, is created new. The old life is gone; a new life emerges! Look at it!

2 Corinthians 5:17

Christ lives in me. The life you see me living is not "mine," but it is lived by faith in the Son of God, who loved me and gave himself for me.

Galatians 2:20

Chapter 1
What does it mean to make something the center of our lives?

Logan knew exactly what he wanted to do first at Wheel World: ride the Rubber Bumpers. He felt both nervous and happy as he stood in line with his dad.

Logan had wanted to visit Wheel World for a long time. Each week when his family drove to church, they passed the amusement park. It looked so fun and exciting! Plus, some of his friends told him it was their favorite place to go.

The line for Rubber Bumpers moved slowly. But Logan knew it would be worth the wait.

Finally, the buzzer sounded for his group's turn. Logan and his dad climbed into one of the small, low cars. His dad helped him put on a safety belt. Then his dad secured his own belt in the seat next to Logan.

"Here we go!" Logan shouted as the light on the wall turned green.

"Whoo-hoo!" his dad exclaimed as they whirled and twirled and bumped around with the other cars.

When the light turned red, the boy asked his dad if they could go again.

"Not right now," Dad replied. "Let's go see what else is at Wheel World."

The pair spent the morning going to each part of the park. Logan noticed that to get from place to place in the park, they often had to go through the center, past a large statue of a man.

The bronze man seemed friendly. He had a big smile on his face and a toy truck in his hand.

After a few roller coasters and a Chicken Pothole Pie for lunch, Logan asked his dad for some ice cream. His dad happily got him a cone. Then the two of them started out in search of some new places in the park.

As they walked, Logan licked his ice cream quickly to stop it from melting down the side of his cone. That's when he saw the statue again.

"Hey, Dad!" he called ahead. "Who's that guy?"

His father turned to look at the tall figure in the middle of the park. "That? Oh. That's Mr. B. He created this whole theme park." His dad pointed all around where he and Logan stood.

Dad continued, "All of Wheel World was his idea. The rides, the car picture on the shirt we bought you, and even the special flavor of ice cream you are eating. Your ice cream is called Smooth Street."

"Why is the statue right here?" Logan wondered aloud.

"This is Central Hub Park." Logan's dad took his hand and led him over to a map. The boy could see the shape of a car wheel on the map.

The middle of the map said, "You Are Here." The boy's father pointed to all the sidewalks going out from the statue.

"Mr. B loved cars," Logan's dad explained. "Trucks, too! So he created this place to look like a wheel. Nothing would be in Wheel World without its inventor, so some engineers put a statue of him in the middle of the park. They wanted to honor Mr. B and remember that he's important to this place."

"Ohhh. That makes sense!" Logan said.

For the rest of the afternoon, Logan thought about Mr. B. He realized how thankful he was to Mr. B for creating Wheel World. It must have cost the man a lot of time and money to make such a special place for people to enjoy and spend time together.

As Wheel World was about to close that evening, Logan and his dad passed the statue one last time on their way to the parking lot.

Logan waved at the friendly-faced figure in Central Hub Park. "Bye, Mr. B!" the boy said. "Thanks for *everything*!"

When something is at **the center**, that means it is the main or most important thing. (Hint: "Central" is a word that means "at the center.")

Think about these things from the story you read:

What was at the center of Wheel World?

Why was it important?

Now consider your own life:

What are some things that are central in your life? Think about the stuff that's really important to you. Take a minute to consider your answers. You could even write them down on a piece of paper.

Did you say something like your family or your house or even a toy? That makes sense! Those are good things! And God wants you to enjoy them. But here's what we're going to learn: Even very good things can never be as important in your life as Jesus, because Jesus is the very best thing.

Jesus is the center of everything in our whole world. Jesus also wants to be the center of your life. Why? Because he loves you and wants to show you his plan for the best way to live. Jesus' plans are always great, and he has done some pretty great things already.

Next, we'll explore more about what makes Jesus so great.

Chapter 2
Why make Jesus the center of our lives?

A long, long time ago, Jesus came into the world God made because things here had gotten messed up.

Have you ever noticed how many things are sad and wrong in the world? That's because the first people tried to do life without God. All this happened way back in the beginning of the Bible (Genesis 3).

When the first people tried to do life without God, they decided not to do what God had told them. A word for this is **sin**. Sin broke not just the relationship between God and people but everything else in the world too. It's why this world has sickness and sadness and death. Humans couldn't fix what was broken. Only God could. So for many, many years, people waited for everything to be made right again.

> **Sin** is when we do the opposite
> of what God wants us to do.

At the perfect time, God the Father sent Jesus to be the Savior of the world. The word **Savior** means "someone who saves or rescues." Luke 19:10 says, "The Son of Man came to seek and save those who are lost" (NLT). Jesus came to fix our relationship with God and show us the better way to live. Because of Jesus, we can also be sure that there will be a day with no more sadness, sickness, or death.

What are some other great things about Jesus? Let's look at them together.

Jesus was there at Creation!

In the beginning, the Word was already there. The Word was with God, and the Word was God. He was with God in the beginning. All things were made through him. Nothing that has been made was made without him.

John 1:1-3, NIrV

How many times does "the Word" appear in the passage above? ☐

Besides meaning "the Bible," **the Word** is also a name for Jesus. Everything was made through Jesus—even you!

Jesus is the Son of God.

As soon as Jesus came out of the water, he saw the sky open and the Holy Spirit coming down to him like a dove. A voice from heaven said, "You are my own dear Son, and I am pleased with you."

Mark 1:10-11, CEV

The voice from heaven in this passage is God the Father. Jesus wasn't just his Son. The Bible tells us that Jesus was his *dear* Son and he pleased his Father.

Jesus gives us a full life that lasts forever.

"A thief is only there to steal and kill and destroy. I came so they can have real and eternal life, more and better life than they ever dreamed of."

John 10:10

Jesus is the one talking in the verse you just read. Put your finger on each of these words as you say them aloud: "real," "eternal," "more," "better." Jesus offers us the kind of life no one else can give. Better than we can imagine!

> **Jesus has power over everything.**
> God raised him from death and set him on a throne in deep heaven, in charge of running the universe, everything from galaxies to governments, no name and no power exempt from his rule. And not just for the time being, but *forever*. He is in charge of it all.
> Ephesians 1:20-21

Look at the list below. Circle or point to the things Jesus is in charge of running:

- my town
- my country
- the world
- the universe
- my school
- my church

Did you end up picking all the things on the list? I bet you did—because Jesus "is in charge of it all" just like the verse says. Now close your eyes and picture Jesus in the middle of everything he's in charge of. What did the picture in your mind look like?

> **Jesus is always with us.**
> "Teach these new disciples to obey all the commands I have given you. And be sure of this: I am with you always, even to the end of the age."
> Matthew 28:20, NLT

Jesus is talking to his followers in this verse. If you have chosen to follow Jesus, he's talking to you, too. He is always with you.

> Have you made a choice to follow Jesus? If you have, then you are a Christian. The word **Christian** means "a follower of Christ." If you haven't become a Christian yet and you want to learn more about what that means, check out pages 133–135.

● ● ● ● ●

Wow! Jesus is a lot of amazing things!

Because of who Jesus is, you can trust him. You can believe that he cares about every part of your life. Even though humans make mistakes, Jesus is perfect and able to do anything.

He is able to comfort you when you feel sad. He can teach you what to do. He even knows what will happen before it happens!

Have you ever played a sport where you had a coach to help you? Or maybe you've seen coaches giving players directions during a game. Jesus wants you on his team!

He's the biggest, best, and most skilled coach there is. He's smart. He knows all the rules, and he's always going to help you win.

When you choose to make Jesus the center of your life, you let him be in charge of your life. You let him tell you what needs to be done, and you trust he's giving you good directions because he cares about everything that happens to you.

There is just one problem.

When people chose to sin in the beginning of the Bible, it became easy for all of us to do bad things. We don't like to be told what to do. We don't want to obey. We may not want to try to do the right thing, because it sounds hard.

In the next chapter, we'll discover some of the differences between our old life of sin and the new life Jesus offers when we make him the center.

Chapter 3
What keeps us from making Jesus the center?

Let's read this verse together:

Anyone united with the Messiah gets a fresh start, is created
new. The old life is gone; a new life emerges! Look at it!
2 Corinthians 5:17

Some of the words in this verse might be new to you. Here's what
they mean:

- **united:** connected
- **the Messiah:** a name for Jesus
- **emerges:** appears

Second Corinthians is a letter. A man named Paul wrote these
words to a group of people in a city called Corinth. Paul had made
a lot of bad choices. In fact, he had hurt some of God's people. But
then Jesus spoke to Paul one day. Paul changed his ways and started
his new life in Jesus!

Paul was so excited by his new life that he wanted to share the
Good News about Jesus with everyone.

Let's take a look at some of the other verses written in Paul's letter. Read 2 Corinthians 5:14-18 in a Bible. (If you don't know how to look this up, try asking an adult in your house or someone you know who likes to read the Bible.)

After reading the verses, think about these questions:

Who did Jesus die for?

What words in these verses tell us that followers of Jesus have changed?

You probably noticed that the words "old" and "new" are used in 2 Corinthians 5:17.

The "old life" is when we give in to sin and do the opposite of what God wants us to do. We do what we want instead of following his plan for the best way to live. Some examples of sin are lying, cheating, disobeying, being mean, and being selfish.

What are some other kinds of sin you can think of?

The "new life" is the new way to live that Jesus gives us. When we keep Jesus at the center of our lives, we find ourselves changing and acting in ways that are good. Some examples are being honest, obeying, being kind, and caring about others.

What else can you think of that comes from a new life in Jesus?

Paul wrote some other words about the old life and the new life. Check out these verses.

OLD	NEW
Romans 6:14—Don't let sin keep ruling your lives. You are ruled by God's undeserved grace and not by the Law. (CEV)	Ephesians 4:23-24—You were taught to be made new in your thinking. You were taught to start living a new life. It is created to be truly good and holy, just as God is. (NIrV)
Ephesians 4:22—You were taught not to live the way you used to. You must get rid of your old way of life. (NIrV)	Ephesians 4:29—Let no evil talk come out of your mouths, but only what is useful for building up, as there is need, so that your words may give grace to those who hear. (NRSV)
Colossians 3:9—Don't lie to one another. You're done with that old life.	Ephesians 4:31—Get rid of all hard feelings, anger and rage. Stop all fighting and lying. Don't have anything to do with any kind of hatred. (NIrV)
1 Peter 1:14—Don't lazily slip back into those old grooves of evil, doing just what you feel like doing. You didn't know any better then; you do now.	Romans 6:11—You are dead to sin and alive to God. That's what Jesus did.

As you think about these verses . . .

What is the old life like?

What is the new life like?

Write any words you can find in the verses that tell what these two kinds of lives are like. You can also add your own words to the lists.

OLD	NEW

Now ask yourself this question:

Where does this new life come from?

How can you live this new life?

All of us sin and make mistakes. Even people who follow Jesus! Jesus gives us a way to live this new life with God even when we mess up: confessing our sins to him. When we **confess**, we admit to Jesus that we did something wrong (or didn't do something right). Then we tell him we're sorry.

The Bible says that Jesus forgives us for our sins if we confess them (Psalm 86:5; 1 John 1:9). That is how we can move from living the old life to living the new life.

Take a moment to think about anything you want to tell Jesus right now. Is there something you have done wrong, or a situation where you didn't do the right thing when it was important? Confess that to Jesus. Here are some words you can say as you talk with him. Write your own below.

Jesus, I am sorry for _____.
    Please forgive me.
    I want to follow you every day.
    Please help me.

Confessing is good for us! It helps us put away the old life and live in our new life in Jesus. Confessing is not a thing you do only once. Sometimes you might need to say you are sorry to Jesus a few times a day.

He will always forgive you, and he is ready to show you the better way to live.

Chapter 4
What does a life with Jesus at the center look like?

- "Just have faith."
- "I'm going to take a leap of faith."
- "You've got to keep the faith."
- "O ye of little faith."

Have you ever heard any of these sentences?

Faith is a popular subject. The word "faith" appears in the Bible a lot. Many Christians also talk about faith. There's a good reason why—it is very important. **Having faith in Jesus** means trusting in him *and* obeying him.

When was a time when you heard the word "faith" used?

What does the word "faith" make you think of?

Let's read this verse together. This verse is from a letter written by Paul. Look for the word "faith" in the verse.

Christ lives in me. The life you see me living is not "mine," but it is lived by faith in the Son of God, who loved me and gave himself for me.
Galatians 2:20

Now think about your answers to these questions:

Who lives in Paul?

How does Paul live his life?

Who is the Son of God? (Hint: If you don't remember, go back to chapter 2.)

What two things did the Son of God do?

Paul wrote this letter to Christians in a place called Galatia (pronounced Guh-LAY-shuh). Some of the church leaders in Galatia didn't like that the people chose to make Jesus the center of their lives. These leaders wanted the people to keep following the same rules they had obeyed for many, many years. They wanted the rules to be the most important part of the people's lives.

It isn't that the rules of the leaders were bad. It's just that the rules couldn't give them the life that Jesus does. Jesus died and rose again to give us freedom. The church leaders in Galatia didn't realize that.

Paul knew the difference. He had tried living only by the rules before he met Jesus. It didn't work. So he chose to live "by faith" instead. Remember, having faith in Jesus is trusting *and* obeying Jesus.

Paul trusted and obeyed Jesus because Jesus loved Paul and gave up his life for Paul.

In fact, Jesus loves all of us and gave up his life for all of us.

Do you think having faith in Jesus is easy or hard?

What makes you think so?

Trusting in Jesus is going to be easier on some days than others. It's easy to believe Jesus is alive and taking care of you when things are going well.

Maybe you scored a goal in your soccer game, and everyone cheered for you. The cheers felt good. Or maybe you got a special gift from a best friend. The gift reminds you that you are loved.

But what about bad days? Maybe someone you care about is very sick and about to die. Or maybe someone close to you said something awful and mean.

Bad days might cause us to ask where Jesus is and why he isn't helping. We might wonder, *Where are you, Jesus? I made the choice to follow you, but it seems like you don't care.*

Sometimes bad times in our lives continue for weeks and months. How can you keep having faith in Jesus then?

If you haven't experienced hard times, you will. Sadness and pain happen to everyone. We have sadness and pain because sin is part of our world.

But we can get through anything because Christ lives in us. That means he is part of our lives all the time. He is part of our lives whether we feel like he is there or not.

What kind of life do we have when we live by faith? Romans 1:17 tells us, "Scripture has said all along: 'The person in right standing before God by trusting him really lives.'"

What do you think it means to "really live"?

Some people think that really living is having everything you want, like a nice car, a new phone, or lots of money. The problem with all these things is that they don't last. They can break or get lost or be stolen.

Jesus gives us more. Much more!

The life Jesus offers us begins now and goes on forever. **Forever** means "going on and on without stopping." It's not there one day and gone the next day. It can't be taken away from us. It can't be broken, lost, or stolen.

Jesus helps us live like no one else because the things Jesus gives us—peace, joy, love, hope, belonging to him—are better than things that will make us happy for one day. We can receive what he wants to give us when we trust and obey him.

Chapter 5
How do we make Jesus the center of our lives?

Doesn't living by faith seem like a pretty hard thing to do? So how can we do it? Well, we are able to be faithful because Jesus was faithful first!

Being **faithful** means being worthy of trust. Jesus is worthy of trust because he never changes and because he does what he says he will do. We can count on him.

Look for the word "faithful" in this verse:

But Lord, you are a God who is tender and kind.
    You are gracious.
You are slow to get angry.
    You are faithful and full of love.
Psalm 86:15, NIrV

What does this verse say about God?

What do you know about Jesus that helps you trust him?

We make Jesus the center of our lives when we remember who he is and what he has done.

The Bible is full of things we can learn about God. There are even four whole books about Jesus' life. These books are called the **Gospels**. The titles of the Gospels are Matthew, Mark, Luke, and John. They are the first four books of the New Testament.

Let's read a story about Jesus and his disciples from the Gospel of Mark. The **disciples** were people who followed Jesus everywhere he went.

As evening came, Jesus said to his disciples, "Let's cross to the other side of the lake." So they took Jesus in the boat and started out, leaving the crowds behind (although other boats followed). But soon a fierce storm came up. High waves were breaking into the boat, and it began to fill with water.

Jesus was sleeping at the back of the boat with his head on a cushion. The disciples woke him up, shouting, "Teacher, don't you care that we're going to drown?"

When Jesus woke up, he rebuked the wind and said to the waves, "Silence! Be still!" Suddenly the wind stopped, and there was a great calm. Then he asked them, "Why are you afraid? Do you still have no faith?"

The disciples were absolutely terrified. "Who is this man?" they asked each other. "Even the wind and waves obey him!"

Mark 4:35-41, NLT

Draw a picture of the story in this box or on another piece of paper.

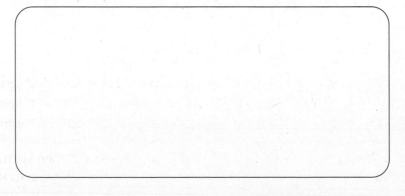

24

Where did this story happen?

The disciples had different feelings about the storm than Jesus did. How did the disciples feel in these verses?

What did Jesus do when he woke up?

Even though the disciples went everywhere with Jesus, they still had a hard time trusting him. They didn't know everything about who he was during a lot of their time with him.

What questions did Jesus ask?

What question did the disciples ask?

What did the disciples learn about Jesus that day?

The disciples were scared to trust Jesus until they saw that Jesus calmed the waves. Living a life with Jesus at the center doesn't mean we will always make the right choices. It also doesn't mean we will know the answer to every problem. But we can trust that Jesus does.

When we are upset, we can go to Jesus for peace. When we are afraid, we can remember that Jesus is strong. When we are sad, we can remember that Jesus can give us joy. When we don't know what choice to make, we can ask Jesus to make us wise.

Making Jesus the center of our lives means we go to him over and over. We tell him that we need him. We believe that he is the only one who can help us with every part of our lives.

From the Author

When my daughter Kaelyn was three, she got all her necklaces tangled up into a big ball. She sat for a long time and tried to figure out how to get the knots apart. She was very patient but couldn't get even one necklace to come loose.

Finally, she handed the jumbled ball of beads and chains to me. She declared, "Here. Your turn." She walked away, trusting that I could fix the giant mess for her. She didn't stay to see how I worked the tangles out. She simply believed that I was the best person to fix her problem.

It took a while, but I did get the scrambled chains pulled apart. I laid all the necklaces out, and Kaelyn was full of joy when she saw them. I was glad I could help her because I love her. I remember thinking, *That is how Jesus must feel about me.* He wants me to come to him for everything I need.

Think about who Jesus is and what he has done for you. If you want to make him the center of everything in your life, ask him to help you. Let him know that you trust him and want to obey him.

How can you make Jesus the center of your life today?

In the next section, we will discover more about obeying Jesus and how that keeps us moving in our life with God.

Section 2
obey Jesus!

"The person who knows my commandments and keeps them, that's who loves me. And the person who loves me will be loved by my Father, and I will love him and make myself plain to him."

John 14:21

So here's what I want you to do, God helping you: Take your everyday, ordinary life—your sleeping, eating, going-to-work, and walking-around life—and place it before God as an offering. Embracing what God does for you is the best thing you can do for him.

Romans 12:1

Chapter 6
What does it mean to obey?

Ava tried to grab her suitcase, blanket, and pillow all at once. It was a lot to carry up the hill to her cabin. She was afraid the items would get dusty or full of pine needles.

Her counselor, Tasha, took one of the handles on the suitcase. "Here, let me help you," Tasha offered.

Ava followed Tasha up the steepest part of the path. She smiled as they walked up the familiar path because she had stayed at Camp ACT before. ACT stood for All Come Together. The young girl waved when she spotted a camper who was in her cabin last summer. The other girl smiled and waved back. She called out, "See you at dinner!"

Once inside the cabin, Ava chose her bunk bed and positioned her things in the right places. She remembered where everything should go.

Everything about her cabin felt familiar and comforting. Plus, it helped that she knew where to find everything at the camp—the main lodge where dinner was served, the boathouse at the lake where you could rent canoes, the craft tent just to the right of the boathouse.

As more campers arrived, Ava saw familiar faces and helped new campers get settled. From the cabin's porch, she pointed out the best places around Camp ACT to have fun.

Finally, the bell rang out across the cabins. It was time for dinner!

The campers piled into the dining hall. As the kids found their seats, they sang the camp theme song. Ava smiled. It was time for all the good things she had been waiting on for months. This was going to be the best week of the year!

The sun was still up after dinner. All the campers were invited to find a seat on the wooden benches just outside the lodge. The porch lights shone down on a list of words painted on a giant piece of wood.

Ava knew what was about to happen. The camp commander, Mr. Sandoval, was going to talk to them about what it meant to be a Camp ACT camper.

The list said:

A Camp ACT camper is . . .

- caring
- kind
- giving
- loyal
- honest
- wise
- humble

"Everyone is here to have fun!" said Mr. Sandoval. "You can play as hard as you can in every game and activity. But every camper needs to remember the list of what a Camp ACT camper is. Whatever you do, you do it as a Camp ACT camper."

Mr. Sandoval also explained that there were other signs around the camp. These signs had more specific rules to obey. He continued, "Every list of rules has this line at the top: 'Remember what a Camp ACT camper is, and please follow these rules.'"

As the children were dismissed, Ava thought about how much she loved being part of the camp. She felt like she belonged, and that made her want to be the best Camp ACT camper she could be!

Ava was right. It was the best week of her year. She made up cheers with her friends about being ACT campers. They proudly wore their camp T-shirts and sang the theme song as loud as they could at each meal. Tasha even taught them some motions to go with the song lyrics.

At the end of the week, Ava's family arrived to pick her up from camp. She happily showed them her cabin and some things she had made at the craft tent. She talked about zip-lining through the trees and seeing a giant hawk fly over her head on a hike.

As she walked to her car, Ava glanced back at the list outside the lodge. She wanted to remember those words so she could be an ACT camper all the time.

How did Ava feel about being at Camp ACT?

What did Mr. Sandoval show the kids first?

What were the campers supposed to do before following the rules on other signs?

What are some places in your life where you feel you belong? If you don't have any yet, what would a place like that be like?

Do those places have rules to obey? Why do you think that is?

Before pointing out the rules, Mr. Sandoval brought the kids together and helped them understand who they were—they were Camp ACT campers! Being a camper is much bigger than just being obedient and doing the right things while at camp. Mr. Sandoval wanted the kids to feel as if they belonged there.

In our lives, Jesus is the one in charge of all things. When we choose to follow Jesus, he says we are his children. We are loved and set apart from the rest of the world. Because we belong to him, he gives us certain rules to obey. Sometimes these rules are also called commands.

Obeying Jesus' commands is part of faith. Remember, when we live by faith in Jesus, we both trust him *and* obey him.

Let's find out more about obeying Jesus!

Chapter 7

What does Jesus want us to obey?

Let's read this verse together:

"The person who knows my commandments and keeps them, that's who loves me. And the person who loves me will be loved by my Father, and I will love him and make myself plain to him."
John 14:21

Some of these words might be new to you. Here's what they mean:

- **Commandments** is another word for "commands."
- To **keep commandments** means "to obey."

The verse you just read is from the Gospel of John. John was one of Jesus' disciples. In fact, the Bible says that John was "the one Jesus loved" (John 20:2).

In John 14, Jesus was telling his disciples what would happen after he went back to heaven. The disciples didn't know yet that Jesus was going to die, rise again, and then go to heaven to be with God the Father.

Read John 14:15-21 in a Bible. (Remember, if you don't know how to look this up, you can try asking an adult in your house or someone you know who likes to read the Bible.)

After reading the verses, answer these questions:

If you love Jesus, how will you show it?

Why is the Father sending the Spirit after Jesus is gone?

What promise does Jesus make in verse 18?

What will Jesus do for the person who obeys his commands?

Go back and count how many times the word "love" is used in John 14:21.

Before Jesus spoke these words to his disciples, he had spent years with them. He loved them and had shown them how to love others. They trusted him and knew that he wanted what was best for them. So it wasn't strange to know that if they loved him they would obey what he taught them.

When we become Christians, we start a relationship with Jesus too. As we live by faith and learn more about who Jesus is, we will want to follow his commands.

In one of his letters, John calls those who believe in Jesus "children of God" (1 John 3:1). That is why Jesus says he's not going to leave the disciples on their own once he is gone. They are God's children! God was going to send the Helper to be with his children. Another name for **the Helper** is the Holy Spirit.

Now let's go back and look at the word **commandments**. When people hear this word, they often think of the Ten Commandments that God gave to his people near the beginning of the Bible. You might even know some of these commands. (You can read the whole list in Exodus 20:1-17.)

God gave these rules to his people, the Israelites, after he rescued them from being slaves in Egypt. The Israelites had nothing of their own. No land, no food, and not even anything to drink! God told them he had a special land for them. They would need to journey there.

But before they got too far, he wanted to let them know who they were as his people. He did this by calling them his own. Then he gave them the Ten Commandments to tell them how to act because they belonged to him.

Here are some of the words God spoke to his people:

> "You'll know that I am GOD, *your* God who brings you out from under the cruel hard labor of Egypt. I'll bring you into the land that I promised . . . and give it to you as your own country. *I AM* GOD."
> Exodus 6:7-8

All the lands around the Israelites had their own rules and ways to run their countries, just like there are probably rules and laws to follow in the country you live in! God gave his people something of their own. They could say, "We are God's children. Because we are his children, these are the rules we will obey."

Jesus did a similar thing when he chose his followers while he was on earth. And we are also Jesus' disciples if we've chosen to follow him. So he tells us to obey his rules if we love him.

How are Jesus' commands different from other rules in our world?

A really amazing thing about Jesus is that he doesn't make us guess his commands. His commands aren't like a riddle where we have to figure out the answer.

Have you ever looked at really hard instructions to a game or activity? Maybe you were given a tough project and you didn't know how to do it or where to begin. How did you feel?

That feeling is the opposite of how Jesus makes us feel. And if we ever do feel like it's too hard to understand or follow Jesus' commands, we can always ask him to show us what he means and how to obey him. He will use all kinds of things to help us, including the Bible, our families, and our friends.

What or who helps you understand Jesus and his commands?

Take a moment to thank Jesus for making himself plain so that you can obey him. Tell him anything else you want to say about understanding his commands and following his ways.

Chapter 8
Why do we obey Jesus?

In the last chapter we talked about how Jesus gives commands because we belong to him and he loves us. Jesus' commands help us do what's best for us.

In the Gospels, Jesus tells his followers he's the Good Shepherd (John 10:11-18). Shepherds keep their sheep safe. They move them away from other animals that could hurt them, like wolves. Shepherds also lead their sheep to where they can find food and water.

When sheep aren't out grazing with a shepherd nearby, the shepherd places them in a pen for safety. The pen doesn't just keep the wolves out. The pen keeps the sheep from accidentally wandering off. If a sheep walks away from the flock, she could get hurt or fall off a cliff.

Jesus' commands are like the edges or wall of that pen. He shows us the boundaries where we are most able to stay away from harm and stay alive. Remember, Jesus is the one who shows us how to "really live" (Romans 1:17).

Listen to the words a man named David used to describe God as his Shepherd:

GOD, my shepherd!
   I don't need a thing.
You have bedded me down in lush meadows,
   you find me quiet pools to drink from.
True to your word,
   you let me catch my breath
   and send me in the right direction.
Psalm 23:1-3

Did you notice all the things the Shepherd does to bring life to his sheep? Go back through the verses and underline or put your finger on the things God does as our Shepherd.

You might have noticed . . .

- The sheep don't need anything.
- The Shepherd takes them to meadows to eat.
- The Shepherd takes them to quiet pools to drink.
- The Shepherd lets the sheep catch their breath and rest.
- The Shepherd shows them the right way to go.

That's what Jesus' commands do for us. His words show us the right things to do and the correct ways to go so that we can stay near him and the flock.

We have the choice to obey Jesus or not. Disobeying him is a sin. Sin leads to death (Romans 6:23). Sin is part of our old life.

Disobeying our Shepherd is like going out of the pen. It's unsafe. It could mean death. A sheep might go out and not know it. Or a sheep might want to see what it's like away from the flock and run away.

But Jesus, our Shepherd, always gives us a way back to his care. Even if we disobey him, he calls us back. Jesus said that his sheep know his voice (John 10:4). They listen for his instructions so they can follow him. Sheep will never listen to a stranger's voice. Why would they? They can't trust a stranger to keep them safe. They don't know the stranger.

Jesus called these strangers "sheep rustlers" because they want to steal the sheep away from their true sheperd (John 10:8). They scare the sheep and cause them to scatter or run away. They don't care about the sheep at all.

What are some differences between our Shepherd, Jesus, and the "sheep rustlers"?

What might happen to the sheep if they did listen to a "sheep rustler"?

What do you think the voice of the Good Shepherd sounds like? Why do you think that?

Have you ever gotten separated from your parents or a person who was taking care of you? If so, you were probably looking everywhere for them. Running around and feeling scared. You might not know it, but you were probably also listening for their voice. Their voice is the one that you know.

It's the same with Jesus. The more we learn about him, through his Word and through others who know him, the more his voice will be familiar to us. We won't want to be away from him. We will want to be closer and closer to Jesus.

Why? Because we will trust Jesus. We will want to do everything he tells us.

Look up Psalm 23 in your own Bible. (Hint: If you open a Bible to the middle, you will find the book of Psalms.) Read the whole chapter, verses 1 through 6.

Close your eyes and imagine Jesus as your Shepherd right next to you. Imagine he is caring for you and leading you. Then, talk to Jesus as your Shepherd. If you don't know what to say, you can use these words:

Jesus, please be my Shepherd. I trust you with everything. I want to obey you. I want to be near you always.

Chapter 9
How do we obey Jesus?

Let's read this verse together:

> So here's what I want you to do, God helping you: Take your everyday, ordinary life—your sleeping, eating, going-to-work, and walking-around life—and place it before God as an offering. Embracing what God does for you is the best thing you can do for him.
> Romans 12:1

Some of these words might be new to you. Here's what they mean:

- **ordinary:** common; regular
- **offering:** a gift
- **embracing:** accepting; welcoming

The book of Romans is in the New Testament. It's another letter written by Paul. Can you guess who he wrote it to? He sent it to the Christians living in Rome—the Romans!

To understand the verse at the beginning of this chapter, we need to look at a few verses before Romans 12.

Read Romans 11:33-36.

What do these verses say about God?

What is your favorite thing about God from these verses?

Okay, now we can look at Romans 12:1. Put your finger on the first word of the verse (either in your Bible or at the beginning of this chapter).

That first word is telling us to pay attention to what's next. Paul is getting ready to give an instruction to obey. Now put your finger on the first mention of God in this verse.

Think about this question:

Who is going to help us with the things we do for God?

We aren't alone in obeying God. He gives us help. Remember, that is why the Holy Spirit was sent to us!

Next Paul tells what we can do for God since he did so much for us. We are to give all the parts of our ordinary lives to God.

Some ordinary things we do each day are eating and sleeping. Many people go to work. Perhaps for you, ordinary things are going to school and playing sports.

The verse also mentions walking around. We go to the store, our school, our church, the local park, and maybe other people's homes. All these are places we can trust and obey God.

What are some ordinary things you do every day?

Let's look back at Romans 12:1, either in your own Bible or on the first page of this chapter. Put your finger on the word "offering."

We are to give God our ordinary lives as an offering.

Have you ever heard the word **offering**? In churches, it's usually talking about the time when people give their money. Perhaps someone plays a special song while people put money in a plate or basket.

But an offering can be more than money. It can be our time, what we own, or things we are good at, like building or painting. All these things are gifts we can give to God as an offering.

In the Old Testament, people brought things like their animals or their crops (such as fruit or vegetables) as an offering. The Israelites brought the *best* of those things to God.

Learning to give God the best of what we have in our lives is not easy. We like our things, our time, and our money. It's hard to share. Sometimes it's hard to think about anyone but ourselves!

But Paul told us how we can take this ordinary life and offer it to God. Here's the answer from the end of Romans 12:1:

Embracing what God does for you is the best thing you can do for him.

When we think about all God has done for us, we'll want to give everything to God. When we see that everything comes from God, then we'll realize we can trust him with anything!

That means these things are true:

- We can trust God with our feelings, like sadness or joy.

- We can trust him with our time, like what happens tomorrow or what has already happened.

- We can trust him with our things by being willing to share or give gifts to people.

- We can trust him with our talents by practicing things we love, such as drawing or singing.

Here's an idea for how you can remember all this:

Go back to thinking about the ordinary things you do every day. Start at the beginning of the day and go to bedtime. Maybe think of it like this:

- getting dressed
- eating breakfast
- doing schoolwork
- eating lunch
- playing (with a team, friends, or siblings)

- eating dinner
- putting on pajamas
- brushing teeth
- climbing into bed

Add your own ideas here:

Now pick just one of those things to start offering to God.

Like when you slip on your shoes, you can ask God to guide every step you take that day.

Or when you eat your lunch, thank God for the farmers who grow the food we eat.

Or when you're brushing your teeth, ask God to keep you from saying hurtful things to others.

Once you get used to offering God one part of your life, you might want to add in another thing to your day.

No matter what, God is willing to help you. He's so excited to be part of everything in your ordinary life.

Chapter 10
What happens if I don't obey Jesus?

Once upon a time, there was a man who owned a lot of land and animals. He also had two sons. Those sons knew that one day, everything their father owned would be theirs.

But the younger son didn't want to wait. He wanted to have his part of the property now! He wanted a lot of money so he could go away and spend it on anything he wanted to.

The father said, "Okay." He gave the younger son his part of the property. The young man left to go to another country. In that new place, the son wasted all his money. All of it! There wasn't anything left!

Because the runaway son had no money for food, he became very hungry. He decided to get some work feeding another man's pigs. He was so hungry that he wanted to eat the corncobs in the pig's slop. *Ewww.* But no one would let him do even that!

Then the son remembered something. He thought about his father's servants. His father treated the servants well. They were never hungry!

The young man decided to go home to see if his father would hire him as a servant. He planned to say, "Father, I've sinned against God and you. I shouldn't even be called your son. Please take me on as a servant."

So the son started walking home.

When the son was still a long way away, his father saw him and ran to his long-lost child. He was so happy to see him! He threw his arms around his neck and kissed his boy.

The son began the speech he had practiced: "Father, I've sinned against God and you. I shouldn't . . ."

But the father wasn't listening. He had other plans in mind.

The father called together all his servants. He told them to bring clean clothes. The father put his family ring on the son and gave him sandals. (A good idea because his feet probably hurt from all the walking, huh?)

Then the servants were told to get a roast to make for dinner. Actually, not just dinner—the father wanted a whole feast!

Now remember, the father had two sons. The older son heard the feast happening as he came to the house a little later. The servants told him what was going on. The older son was not happy. He wasn't happy at all. He had stayed home and worked, but no one threw him a party! When he told his father that he was upset, here's what the father said: "This is a wonderful time, and we had to celebrate. This brother of yours was dead, and he's alive! He was lost, and he's found!" (Luke 15:32).[2]

● ● ● ● ●

Being obedient and doing the right thing don't come easily. We don't always want to follow the rules or wait for the right time.

When we disobey Jesus, we are turning away from him just like the younger son who left his father. When we leave the safety of our Shepherd, we are lost.

What could cause us to move away from Jesus? What could cause us to do the opposite of what he wants for us?

It's sin. It's wanting to do what we want when we want it. When we get these ideas, it's called **temptation**. Being tempted isn't wrong. But giving in to temptation and doing the wrong thing is.

Let's think about one of the most well-known commands given to children. Lots of kids know this one! It goes like this: "Children, obey your parents" (Ephesians 6:1, NLT).

Why do you think God tells us to obey our parents?

Another thing God said is to "honor" our parents (Ephesians 6:2-3). That means "to show them respect."

In the story we read, the son did not honor his father. He asked for his money before it was the right time. Later, the son realized he had done wrong. He returned to his father. He confessed his sin. The father knew the son was sorry because the son came back. It was the son's actions, not just his words, that helped the man know his boy had changed. The father welcomed his younger son and celebrated his return.

In chapter 3, we talked about **confessing**. This means admitting when we do something wrong and being sorry about it. Confessing isn't just about saying the right words. It's about changing the way we think. It's about wanting to do the right thing next time.

When we sin, it's important that we tell God we're sorry. When we confess our disobedience to God, he forgives us (1 John 1:9). He welcomes us just like the father did in the story.

When is it hardest for you to be obedient to God? Confess it to him today and ask for his help to obey him.

Take a moment to tell God you are sorry for your sins. Let him know you want to do better next time. Remember, God *always* forgives us when we come to him. Now close your eyes and imagine Jesus welcoming you, hugging you, and celebrating that you have returned to his ways.

Next, we're going to look at God's Word and discover how we can learn more about what Jesus tells us through the Bible. Knowing the Bible more and more helps us obey and love Jesus more.

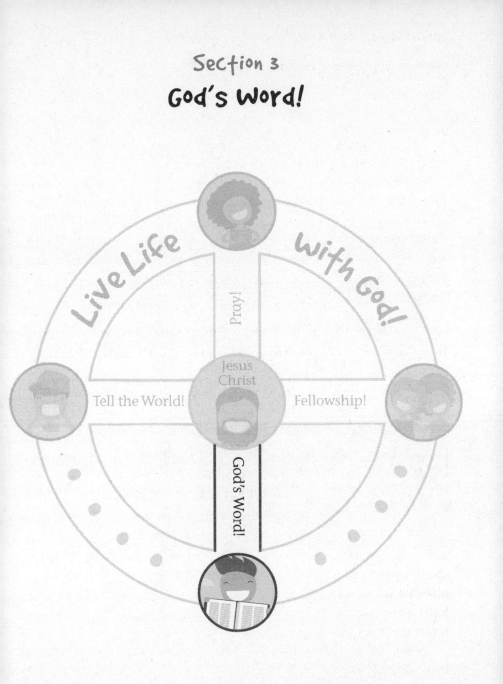

Every part of Scripture is God-breathed and useful one way or another—showing us truth, exposing our rebellion, correcting our mistakes, training us to live God's way.

2 Timothy 3:16

"And don't for a minute let this Book of The Revelation be out of mind. Ponder and meditate on it day and night, making sure you practice everything written in it. Then you'll get where you're going; then you'll succeed."

Joshua 1:8

Chapter 11
What is the Bible?

Kaia rolled the dough quickly so it wouldn't stick to her palms. She placed a small, smooth ball onto a plate.

Her little brother plucked the doughball off the plate. Kaia glanced to the side. She didn't want Aiden to lick the sugar from his fingers (again).

Thankfully, Grandma came over at that moment to direct him. Aiden did his job correctly, dropping the small piece of dough into the bowl of sugar and cinnamon.

Grandma helped Kaia's brother place the dough onto a cookie sheet. Then she had Aiden stand far away as she slid the silver pan into the oven. After setting a timer, Grandma came back to Kaia. Kaia showed her the empty bowl, and they both began to wash the dishes.

A couple of fingers slid up the counter right in front of the sink. The cookies that had already been baked were cooling just inches away from the small fingers.

"Aiden," Grandma called out, "if you want a cookie, all you have to do is ask. Don't sneak."

"Pleeeeease," Aiden begged. Grandma handed him a cookie, and the boy ran off to play with his toys.

Kaia knew what to do now that all the dishes were done. It was time to put away the book that held the famous cookie recipe. These cookies were a family tradition.

Instead of closing the book like she always did, Kaia asked if she could flip through the pages this time.

"Of course!" Grandma exclaimed. "I think you might be surprised by what you find. If you have questions, just ask me."

Questions? Kaia thought. *Why would I have questions?*

The young girl flipped to the front of the book. The first page read, "Dedicated to the Pioneers of First Church, 1884."

There was a black-and-white picture under the words. The image showed men, women, and children of all ages. No one smiled. But Kaia could see kindness in their eyes.

The pages of the book were thin and worn. Kaia was careful as she turned them. Among the contents, Kaia spotted Bible verses, songs, stories, poems, and, of course, recipes.

Beep, beep, beep. The final timer sounded. Grandma pulled the last batch of cookies out. Then she came to sit next to Kaia at the kitchen table.

"Grandma," Kaia asked, "why are there so many dates in here? Also, why is the book full of many different things instead of one thing? I thought there would be more recipes."

"That is a good question," Grandma replied. "This book tells the story of First Church. Your great-great-great-grandparents helped start this church." She flipped back to the picture at the beginning and pointed to a man and woman in the back row.

Grandma continued, "Because God created each person different, each member of the church got to tell the story of the church in their own way—like songs, stories, and recipes. I have a few more books like this one." She pointed to the top shelf in the pantry. "I just get this book out more because it has our special recipe."

"Can I see the other books?" Kaia asked.

"Yes! I'll get them." Grandma loaded the other books into a pile on the table.

For the next hour, Kaia looked over the books with Grandma.

She was surprised to find that she knew a lot of the songs, verses, and stories she read. The young girl had heard them sung at church and told at family gatherings.

Even though Kaia wasn't around when the church was started in 1884, she felt connected to everything she discovered in the books. She knew that this was her history too. She wondered how she could have her own copy of a book like this.

Finally, Kaia and Grandma came to the last book. As they neared the end of the pages, Grandma pointed to some names. Kaia couldn't believe it. Her name was included in one of the books! Her birthdate and the day she was baptized were written beside it.

"Wow! I love these!" Kaia exclaimed. Grandma promised to get Kaia her own copy of the current edition soon. The girl smiled as she bit into one of their cookies.

In addition to the cookie recipe, what was in the books?

How did Kaia know about some of those other things even though she hadn't seen all the books?

Why do you think Kaia wanted her own copy of one of the books?

● ● ● ● ●

What is the Bible? Do you know the answer?

The Bible is a book. But it's not just any book. It's the Word of God.

The Bible starts at the very beginning of history, when God created the world from nothing. You can read all about Creation by opening a Bible to Genesis 1. The word **genesis** means "beginning."

Within the Bible, there are sixty-six smaller books.

The Bible is divided into two parts: The Old Testament and The New Testament.

• The Old Testament has thirty-nine books.
• The New Testament has twenty-seven books.

The Bible tells the history of God's people, the Israelites. It also tells how God planned to save us through Jesus from the moment the first people sinned.

Many different human authors helped write the Bible. Have you heard of Moses or David or Solomon? They wrote parts of the Old Testament. We've already talked about John and Paul. These men wrote parts of the New Testament. There were many other writers too.

The Bible has praise songs to God. It has lists of families who followed God for hundreds of years and stories about what has happened when people have decided not to follow God. God's Word tells when and how Jesus saved us. The Bible tells us everything we need to know to follow God.

Second Timothy 3:17 says, "Through the Word we are put together and shaped up for the tasks God has for us."

Chapter 12
What's so great about the Bible?

Did you know that another word for God's Word is **Scripture**? Let's read this verse together and pay attention to the four ways Scripture is useful. (Hint: It might help you to put your finger on the four ways as you read them.)

> Every part of Scripture is God-breathed and useful one way or another—showing us truth, exposing our rebellion, correcting our mistakes, training us to live God's way.
> 2 Timothy 3:16

Some of these words might be new to you. Here's what they mean:

- **exposing:** showing
- **rebellion:** doing the opposite of what someone in charge wants you to do
- **correcting:** fixing

That verse is from a letter Paul wrote to a young man named Timothy. Timothy was a pastor at the church in a city called Ephesus.

Paul wrote this letter from prison. Some people didn't like Paul telling others about Jesus, so they locked him up. That way Paul couldn't teach anyone else about God.

By the time he wrote to Timothy, Paul had been through a lot of hard things.

Read 2 Timothy 3:10-11 to find out what some of those hard things were. (Remember, if you don't know how to look this up, you can try asking an adult in your house or someone you know who likes to read the Bible.)

What had God done for Paul?

What happens to those who want to follow God?

It's true that those who follow God will have to go through hard things. One of those hard things might be people making fun of you for following Jesus. Not everyone will understand living a life of faith in Jesus and loving God.

How can we know truth? Paul gives Timothy the answer in the next verses. Read 2 Timothy 3:14-15.

What does Paul tell Timothy to keep doing?

What tells us about the salvation we have through Jesus?

Now we get to our verses for today. Read 2 Timothy 3:16-17. **God-breathed** means "given by God." The Holy Spirit helped and guided the people who wrote the Bible (2 Peter 1:21). Every part of every book is from God.

How much of Scripture is God-breathed?

Let's take a look at the four things Paul mentioned about God's Word.

Showing Us Truth

Earlier in 2 Timothy, Paul talked about people who were tricking others into following bad teaching—bad teaching that seemed like it was the truth but wasn't.

Jesus told us that the truth sets people free. In John 8:31-32, Jesus said this to the people who believed in him:

> "You are truly my disciples if you remain faithful to my teachings. And you will know the truth, and the truth will set you free." (NLT)

We can always go to God's Word to see if what we are told is right. The Bible will show us the truth!

Exposing Our Rebellion

Because of sin and our old life, it's sometimes hard to want to obey God. God's Word will **expose** or show us where we are doing things the way *we* want to do them instead of God's way.

Remember the story back in chapter 10 about the son who ran away from home and spent all his money? That was **rebellion**. His father wanted him to wait, but the son wanted to do things his way!

The more you know Scripture, the better you will be able to see the places where your heart wants to rebel. It's like the Bible will be saying, "Warning! Warning! Not following God's ways is going to hurt you!"

Correcting Our Mistakes

When we sin, the Bible tells us how to correct our mistakes and make things right. Remember, the Bible says that God forgives us when we make a wrong choice (1 John 1:9). Here are some words from David that show us what this looks like:

> Then I admitted my sin to you.
>   I didn't cover up the wrong I had done.
> I said, "I will admit my lawless acts to the LORD."
>   And you forgave the guilt of my sin.
> Psalm 32:5, NIrV

And here is how God responded to David:

> I will guide you and teach you the way you should go.
>   I will give you good advice and watch over you with love.
> Psalm 32:8, NIrV

In the Bible, we can read about people who struggled with sin like we do. We can also read what God says about forgiveness.

Training Us to Live God's Way

God doesn't make us guess how to follow him. He guides us by what he has to say in his Word—the Bible!

We can read the way he has for us to live. We can also pray that he will make his way known to us through the Bible. Here are some words you can pray:

> Show me the right path, O LORD;
>   point out the road for me to follow.
> Lead me by your truth and teach me,
>   for you are the God who saves me.
> Psalm 25:4-5, NLT

Chapter 13
How can I read the Bible?

It's pretty amazing that we can actually own and hold our own Bibles. This wasn't always true throughout history. The way to print lots of copies of the Bible wasn't invented until about 1,450 years after Jesus came to earth.

Before the Bible was printed for everyone to read, many people learned God's ways by hearing the leaders of their community read the Bible from scrolls. Scrolls were made from plants or animal skins, and people called **scribes** had to write the Bible onto these scrolls all by hand. Can you imagine that? They must have gotten lots of hand cramps, huh?

Why do you think people took the time to write out the Bible on scrolls?

What do you think it would have been like to only hear the Bible being read by others?

Before people used scrolls, pictures and words were carved on rocks. The first copy of God's commands to Israel was written on large pieces of stone by God himself (Exodus 31:18)!

Just because we have our own Bibles, though, doesn't mean the Bible is the same as other books. The Bible was written a long, long time ago, and sometimes the stories and people and ideas may seem strange to us. But the same Holy Spirit who helped people write the Bible helps us understand as we read it.

Here are some ideas for learning how to read the Bible.

Start Where You Want To

We talked about how there are lots of books within the Bible. The name of the first book, Genesis, means "beginning," but you don't have to start reading the Bible there. The Bible is filled with all kinds of writing. There are historical stories of what God has done through his people. There are psalms, which are like songs and poems. There are powerful messages given by God through prophets. There are letters to churches that show us what it looks like to follow Jesus where we live. The Bible is full of lots to explore. If you feel stuck as you're reading, open to a different place!

Look for What You Know

Some words and sentences in the Bible might be confusing to you. But you will also find words and sentences that you do know. That is a good way for you to start when reading the Bible—look for words you know. God's Word is not meant just for grown-ups. It's meant for everyone. That includes you! And God will show you what he wants you to know as you read.

Use the Numbers

The first Bibles didn't have chapters and verses. People read them from beginning to end, and that made sense to them. Now we have chapters and verses. Chapters and verses help us look things up in the Bible.

Let's talk about how *you* can look things up in the Bible. Since there are sixty-six books inside the Bible, it might feel hard to find where those books are.

Here's a hint: The Old Testament is in the front. The New Testament is in the back.

Now, let's pretend you want to look up a verse in Isaiah, but you have no idea where Isaiah is in the Bible. You can open to the very front of your Bible and look for something called the table of contents. The contents page will list all the books in the Bible and on what page you can find the beginning of a book like Isaiah.

Almost every book of the Bible is divided into chapters. Each chapter starts with a big number. Within the chapters are verses. Each verse has a tiny number next to the first word.

Let's try some of this out right now. Grab a Bible. Open to the book of Genesis. Look for the larger number 1. Then look for the smaller number 3 nearby. That is Genesis 1:3. Now you know how to find verses in the Bible!

> If you don't have an actual Bible to hold,
> there are some apps you can use on a phone
> or a tablet to look up chapters and verses.
> (But be sure to ask a trusted adult
> before downloading anything!)

Look for Clues

If we stick with Genesis 1:3, we'll find some familiar words; it should say something about God and light. That's the verse that tells us God created light. And you probably know some of the other words in the verse, like "said" and "there."

But what if you come to a verse that doesn't make sense? Try to look at the verses around it. Sometimes those give other clues about what's happening in that part of the Bible. It's like if you open a storybook and try to figure out what's going on from a middle page. It doesn't always work! You might have to look at details before—and maybe after—that page to understand what's happening.

Try Different Versions

The Bible was first written in Hebrew and Greek. Can you speak Hebrew or Greek? Not many people can! That's why there are different translations and paraphrases of the Bible. A **translation** changes each word from one language into another. A **paraphrase** says parts of sentences in a different way to help us understand what they might be saying.

In order for the Bible to make sense to other readers, people put it into newer language. Back in the year 1611, King James of England had a new translation of the Bible made. This translation is still around today, but it's in an old form of the English language. If you read it, you will see lots of the words "thee" and "thou."

Since this isn't the way we speak now, it might help you find a different version, like the New Living Translation (also called the NLT), or a paraphrase, like *The Message* (also called the MSG).

Just know that if you can't understand one version of the Bible, there are more to try. An adult you know who likes to read the Bible can help you.

Chapter 14

How can I remember what the Bible says?

Do you know the name of the man who led God's people out of Egypt? His name was Moses. God gave the Ten Commandments and all his laws to Moses so God's people would know how to follow God.

Now, there was only one copy of the commandments for thousands of people to use. How do you suppose the people could remember God's words to them? Well, they memorized the laws. To **memorize** means to learn something so well that you can remember it.

Just before Moses died, God chose a man named Joshua to lead his people into their new land. You might recall that God promised his people that they would journey to a home of their own after leaving Egypt.

Let's read about what God said to Joshua right after Moses died. Open your Bible and read Joshua 1:1-6. (Remember, you can ask an adult to help you. Or you can use the table of contents to see where the book of Joshua is in the Bible.)

What did God tell Joshua to do (verse 2)?

Who was giving the land to the Israelites?

What did God promise to Joshua (verse 5)?

Now let's look at a few more verses. Read Joshua 1:6-9.

What would happen if the people obeyed God's laws?

Let's read verse 8 again because the directions God gives here are important:

"Don't for a minute let this Book of The Revelation be out of mind. Ponder and meditate on it day and night, making sure you practice everything written in it. Then you'll get where you're going; then you'll succeed."
Joshua 1:8

Some of these words or phrases might be new to you. Here's what they mean:

- **Book of The Revelation:** God's law
- **ponder:** to think about
- **meditate on:** to think about over and over
- **succeed:** to do well

God didn't want his people to just know his Word. He wanted them to practice everything it said. Just like faith, knowing God's Word requires action, and that action is obeying what God says in the Bible.

When Jesus came to earth, he showed us how important it is to remember God's words. One time, Jesus went out into the desert. He was very hungry and thirsty and tired. The devil came to the desert too. He tried to trick Jesus into doing some wrong things.

But Jesus knew those things were wrong because he knew God's Word. He even said some of God's laws back to the devil! (If you want to read that awesome story, it's found in Matthew 4:1-11.) Jesus showed us that memorizing God's words helps us do the right thing and obey God.

Another good thing about memorizing Scripture is that we can remember who God is and what he has promised us. God has made many promises. By knowing the Bible well, we can remember those promises no matter where we go. It's easy to forget about God when we are going through hard times, but if we memorize God's Word, he will remind us that he loves us and will take care of us even when things are hard.

From the Author

A few years ago, I got really sick and ended up in the hospital. I had to have surgery. I was really worried and kind of mad that God let me get so sick.

When I woke up from the surgery, my first thoughts were some verses I had memorized. I could hear them over and over. I felt like God was speaking to me through his Word.

I started to cry. I remembered that God loved me. He used his Word to remind me he was there with me. His words comforted me and made me feel so much better. I knew that I could get through the sadness of being sick because he was with me.

You might be wondering if you are supposed to memorize the whole Bible. You can, but you don't have to. You can memorize single verses or whole chapters of the Bible. Check out some of Jesus' words in John 10 or John 14 if you want to learn single verses. If you want to memorize a whole chapter, think about Psalm 1 or Psalm 23.

Here are some other helpful ideas for memorizing Scripture:

- Read the same verse from the Bible every day and night for a week. At the end of the week, see if you have it memorized. If not, do the same thing again for another week.

- Write the verse on a note card. Take the note card wherever you go so you can practice the verse.

- Find a Scripture memory resource like the *Topical Memory System for Kids*. Your church might also have a list of helpful verses to memorize.

Check out more ideas for memorizing the Bible in the back of this book on page 137.

Chapter 15

How does the Bible connect to my everyday life?

Since the Bible is so old, maybe you wonder if it really is for you. Kids don't usually open large, old books to read every day. But God's Word is different. He made it for all his people, no matter when they were born or where they live or how old they are.

The Bible is God's living Word that will be around forever. It is also the book that gives us a new life in him (1 Peter 1:23-25).

Because the Bible will be around forever, that means it matters today. It's not some old book that isn't important anymore. It's also not meant to just sit on a shelf.

The book of Hebrews says that God's Word is "alive and powerful" (Hebrews 4:12, NLT). Paul says that it "teaches us to do what is right" (2 Timothy 3:16, NLT).

Do you see why the Bible is so important to our life of faith? **Living by faith** is listening, trusting, and obeying. When we listen to the Bible, we learn what it looks like to follow Jesus.

Here's what Romans 10:17 says:

Faith comes from hearing the message, and the message is heard through the word about Christ.
Romans 10:17, NIV

What "message" do you think this verse is talking about? (Don't forget that sometimes we need to look at other verses around one verse to see what's happening in that part of the Bible.)

A few verses earlier, Romans 10:13 said that everyone who calls on Jesus will be saved. The "message" is the Good News that Jesus died for our sins and rose again!

Think about these questions:

Has the Bible has helped you in the past? If so, how?

How could the Bible help you in the future?

There is so much good stuff in the Bible that you might learn something new every time you open it to read. People keep learning from the Bible for their whole lives! That is one reason it's good to set a goal to keep reading Scripture and memorizing it too.

Do you know what a goal is? A goal is kind of like a dream, but it's a little different. When you have a goal—something that you want to do—you make a plan and follow steps to get to it.

We might make all kinds of goals in our lives. Like . . .

- This year, I want to learn how to play piano. I will start by taking lessons and practicing every day.

- When I grow up, I want to travel to Paris. I will learn how to speak French.

- I want to read every book in my favorite mystery series. I will get a new one every time I go to the library.

Since goals involve making plans and following steps to get to what you want, let's think about making goals related to the Bible. Remember, God told Joshua to "ponder and meditate on [God's words] day and night" (Joshua 1:8). This means that he wants you to always remember his words. How will you read, use, and memorize the Bible regularly?

Here are some ideas of goals related to the Bible:

- I want to read a whole book of the Bible. I will read five verses every night before bed.

- I want to learn all the books of the Bible in order. I will create a poster with all the names and hang it in my room so I can remember them.

- I want to memorize Psalm 23. I will write it out on a note card and draw pictures to help me remember what it says.

These are just some ways to make goals related to the Bible. You can come up with your own as well. Ask a parent or someone you know who reads the Bible to help you make a goal.

God loves when you learn more and more about him in whatever way you can. He has promised to speak to you in many ways. One way is through the Bible. That's why learning Scripture is not a contest, and it is not something that needs to be hurried. God is happy whenever and however you choose to meet with him through his Word.

Next, we will learn about prayer. Prayer is one way you can respond to God about what he says in the Bible.

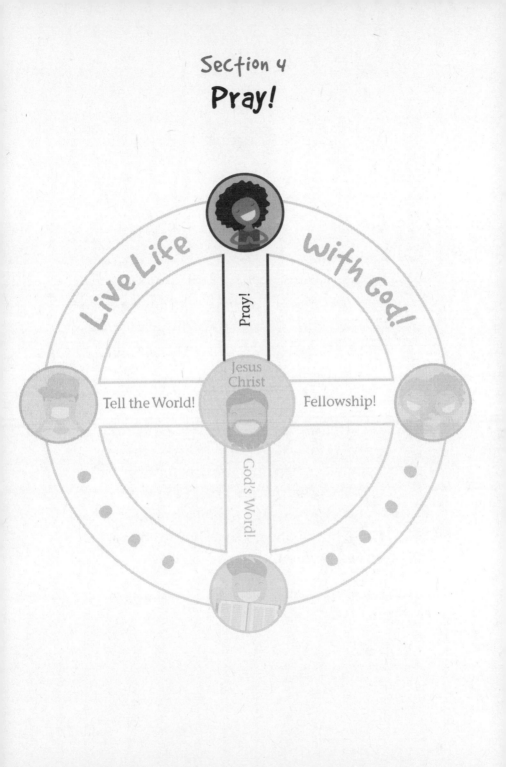

Live Life

with God!

Pray!

Jesus
Christ

Tell the World!

Fellowship!

God's Word!

"But if you make yourselves at home with me and my words are at home in you, you can be sure that whatever you ask will be listened to and acted upon."

John 15:7

Don't fret or worry. Instead of worrying, pray. Let petitions and praises shape your worries into prayers, letting God know your concerns. Before you know it, a sense of God's wholeness, everything coming together for good, will come and settle you down.

Philippians 4:6-7

Chapter 16
What is prayer?

Diego hadn't seen Uncle Leo in fourteen months and four days. The boy knew how long it had been because he was counting the months and days on the family calendar.

And now Diego could stop counting, because his fun uncle was coming home today! Diego had covered that day on the calendar with a bunch of star stickers so he would know when he would get to see Uncle Leo.

In the time Uncle Leo was overseas, he and Diego had found all kinds of fun ways to communicate. They talked on video chats and wrote each other emails. Diego's mom had also let him use her phone to send texts, quotes, and funny pictures.

Diego's favorite thing to receive from Uncle Leo was a card or a letter in the mail. There was nothing like being able to hold something in his hand that his uncle had also held. He liked to see his uncle's handwriting, too.

Occasionally, his uncle would send small things, like stickers, in the cards. That's how Diego had gotten the star stickers he'd used for the calendar. They seemed just right because Uncle Leo called Diego his "superstar."

It had taken time to get ready for Uncle Leo's arrival. Diego's grandmother had made a few pies and several batches of cookies—lots and lots of cookies! There were molasses crinkles, oatmeal chocolate chip cookies, and his uncle's personal favorite, biscochitos. His uncle always said the taste of those cookies reminded him of being home.

Uncle Leo had taught Diego how to say "biscochitos" when he was very young. But Diego could never quite say the whole name. He called them "cheety-yohs" instead.

Food wasn't the only thing the family got ready. Grandpa washed Uncle Leo's car. Diego's mom and dad bought a bunch of balloons and a big sign for the front yard that said "Welcome home!"

Diego was excited. With all the great things happening today, how could he not be?

But deep down, as good as cookies were, Diego was most excited just to be with his uncle. He wanted to tell Uncle Leo about how this last week had been. He'd won the school spelling bee and got a special trophy! Diego also wanted to tell Uncle Leo about how his best friend had broken his arm. Diego was worried about him!

The boy looked forward to hearing his uncle tell amazing stories of the things he had done while he'd been away. He couldn't wait to hear Uncle Leo talk. He never knew how special his uncle's voice sounded until he could no longer hear it every day.

Diego stood by the front window of Grandma and Grandpa's house. He looked and looked for a car. Finally, he saw it. He knew that the car was carrying his uncle. He could see the outline of his head and the hat he always wore.

As soon as the car stopped, the boy bolted out the front door and off the porch. Diego ran through the grass and past the balloons and the colorful welcome sign.

Uncle Leo jumped out of the passenger seat and hugged Diego tight. Uncle Leo continued to hold the boy's hand for a moment while his bags were unloaded.

Of course, there was a lot of excitement all at once. Diego could tell that even as busy as Uncle Leo was hugging people and stuffing cookies into his mouth, he was happy to have his nephew with him.

During dinner, Uncle Leo included Diego in every conversation and called him "superstar."

After a lot of the food had been eaten, Uncle Leo asked Diego about his week. They hadn't talked since the previous week because Uncle Leo had been traveling. Diego told him all about the spelling bee trophy. He also shared about his friend's broken arm.

Uncle Leo promised to take Diego to the store the next day. He planned to help the boy find a special sticker to put on his friend's arm cast.

Diego yawned as his mother told him to go brush his teeth. He really didn't want to leave his uncle's side. But Uncle Leo reminded him, "It's always good to obey your mom, especially since brushing your teeth is part of taking care of yourself. She loves you!"

The boy reluctantly stood up. "Besides," his uncle said, "the faster you go to sleep, the sooner we can do more together tomorrow."

Diego had no problem falling asleep once he placed his head on his pillow that night. Just knowing his beloved uncle was nearby and under the same roof gave him a feeling of comfort.

Home. His uncle was home. They were together again.

What was Diego excited about?

What did Diego's uncle do for him?

How did Diego feel when he went to sleep that night?

● ● ● ● ●

When someone is special to us, we love being near them and talking with them. We want to hear about what's going on in their lives and what's important to them, and we can't wait to tell them all about what's on our mind too.

How does it make you feel when someone special talks with you?

Did you know that God has been talking with people since the beginning of the Bible? You can read one of the first times God and people talked to each other in Genesis 3:8-13. That time, God came looking for Adam and called out to him.

God wants to talk to his people and hear from them too. Talking to God and listening for him is called **prayer**.

When people think of prayer, they often picture being at church with their heads bowed and eyes closed. Lots of people also pray before meals. These are important ways to pray. But there are so many other ways to pray too. We'll explore more about that soon in this book.

The important thing to remember is that prayer is a conversation—talking *and* listening between people and God. It's something we *get* to do! Isn't it special to know that the God of the entire universe wants to hear from you?

How does it make you feel to realize that God wants to talk with you?

He wants your attention. He wants to give you attention too. That's pretty amazing!

Chapter 17
Why do we pray?

"If you make yourselves at home with me and my words are at home in you, you can be sure that whatever you ask will be listened to and acted upon."
John 15:7

Read this verse out loud. Put your fingers on the word "home." The word "home" tells us that we can stay with God. We can feel safe because we are with someone we can trust. Jesus spoke these words to his disciples because he was going to die on the cross soon. He wanted them to know they could receive comfort whenever they went to God because God would listen to them.

Think of a time when you felt safe. Or maybe think of a place that helps you feel safe.

This feeling is what God wants for us when we spend time with him. He cares about you! Because he loves you, he wants you to keep talking to him and listening for him to speak too.

Reading the Bible is one way God speaks to us, so listening to him includes reading the Bible. We can reply to him by saying something back to him about what we've read.

It can be simple, like *Wow, God! I never knew this thing about you! Thanks for telling me that through the Bible.*

It can also be a reply that says we are confused, like *God, something doesn't make sense. Why did this happen? Please help me trust and obey you, even when I don't understand you.*

One great thing about prayer is there are lots of right ways to do it!

How does it make you feel to know you don't have to pray in a certain way?

What would you like to say to God right now?

What does God do when we talk to him? Well, he listens! He tells us this in the verse you read at the beginning of this chapter, which says, "You can be sure that whatever you ask will be listened to and acted upon" (John 15:7).

Similarly, the disciple John also wrote later in the Bible,

> We are confident that he hears us whenever we ask for anything that pleases him. And since we know he hears us when we make our requests, we also know that he will give us what we ask for.
> 1 John 5:14-15, NLT

- **Confident** means "certain" or "sure."
- A **request** is when you ask for something.

You may have heard people use the words **prayer request** around churches or anywhere else Christians get together. It's a common thing people say.

People often share prayer requests with each other and then pray together. They do this because they believe God will hear them *and* also do something to help them.

The end of 1 John 5:15 says, "We also know that he will give us what we ask for" (NLT).

So do we pray just to get whatever we want? Is that why God wants to hear from us? Does he just want to grant our biggest wishes because he loves us?

No. That is not what the verse means.

God gives us what we ask for when it is "anything that pleases him" (1 John 5:14, NLT). That means he will act in a way that is best for us. He will do what is good and safe for us.

What about when bad things are happening in your life? You may wonder if it's okay to ask God to take those things away. It is! He wants you to come to him with those kinds of prayer requests.

But we can't always know what is best for us. God does. He knows so much more than we do because he created us and the world around us. So that means sometimes he will comfort us and give us a way to make the bad thing better. But it may not go away.

No matter what, we can believe that he does care about us during the hard things. He will make the way for us to get through the bad days.

Paul wrote some words to remember when hard things happen:

We can be so sure that every detail in our lives of love for God
is worked into something good.
Romans 8:28

When we pray, we are telling God that we trust him to work everything out for good. He will help us make it through each day, even when it feels like we can't keep going.

Chapter 18
How do I pray?

You already discovered what a prayer request is. A **prayer request** is something you want to ask God for.

Let's talk about a few more kinds of prayers.[3] Hopefully these will give you even more ideas about talking with God.

Praise

Another word for praise is "worship." When we **praise** God, we remember who he is and the things he has done. Then we tell him those things. A good way to start a prayer of praise is with these words:

God, you are _____.

(Think about who God is—loving, kind, forgiving, creative, amazing, and so on.)

OR

God, you have _____.

(Think about what God has done for you or other people in your life, such as helping, saving, and leading.)

Here are some words from Psalm 145:2-3 that are another example of praising God:

Every day I will praise you.
   I will praise your name for ever and ever.
LORD, you are great. You are really worthy of praise.
   No one can completely understand how great you are. (NIrV)

Thanksgiving

When you hear the word "thanksgiving," you might think of a holiday where you eat lots of food. But when we pray with thanksgiving, we are thanking God for, well, everything! Sounds pretty easy, right?

And God has given us so much. Here are some things you can thank him for: friends, family, food, your school, your clothes. Or anything else you can think of! Every good gift comes from God (James 1:17). The Bible tells us to "always give thanks to God the Father for everything" (Ephesians 5:20, NIrV).

Intercession

Intercession (pronounced in-ter-SESH-un) is kind of a big word. It simply means "praying for other people." A prayer of intercession asks God to help someone else.

Have you ever felt sad or worried about someone else and didn't know what to do to help them? You can pray for them. God knows what the people we care about need even more than we do. We can trust him to comfort others and lead them in just the right way.

Here are some words that Paul wrote to the church in Ephesus. He's telling them to pray for each other:

Pray hard and long. Pray for your brothers and sisters. Keep your eyes open. Keep each other's spirits up so that no one falls behind or drops out.
Ephesians 6:18

Keeping each other's spirits up means letting others know they will be okay. They will be okay because God cares about them. Another word for this is **encouragement**.

Confession

Do you remember what **confess** means? It means admitting we've done something wrong.

You might also remember that confession isn't just about saying the right words. It's about being sorry and telling God we want to change the wrong ways we think and act.

When we confess our sins, do you remember what God does for us? He forgives us (1 John 1:9). That means he listens to us and he does something for us—he forgives!

● ● ● ● ●

Just like there are different kinds of prayers, there are also different ways to pray.

People can pray quietly or out loud. Prayer can be done when you are alone or when you are with other people. Prayer can also be planned out or said right when you think of it.

Sometimes people like to pray verses from the Bible because it gives them something to say when they can't think of words. There are verses all over the Bible that can be prayers. You can even turn verses you memorize into prayers like this:

God, help me embrace what you do for me. I know it's the best thing I can do for you. (This prayer comes from the last part of Romans 12:1, which we looked at in chapter 9 of this book!)

You don't need to *say* prayers either. You can write them or sing them! That is what most of the book of Psalms is—a book of poetic songs to God. Psalm 146:1-2 talks about singing to God as long as we live!

There are other fun ways to pray, like drawing or going on prayer walks. One of my friends likes to draw when she prays. She's usually not making pictures. It's more like shapes and squiggles. But, again, there are many right ways to pray, so it's okay if you want to draw a picture while you pray. Some people pray while walking. Walking helps them think about the journey God is leading them on.

You might enjoy going on a **prayer walk**, where you pray for the area where you are walking, like your neighborhood, city, or church. (Just be sure to go with a trusted adult or get permission if you are going out on a prayer walk. This kind of praying is best done in groups.)

What are some ways you've prayed before?

What new way of praying would you like to try?

How can you try out that new way this week?

Chapter 19
What happens when I pray?

Have you ever gotten a puzzle or craft kit and been unsure how it would all fit together to make the picture on the box? Have you ever given up because you didn't know how to start?

When we bring our prayers to God, we can't always see how things will turn out. But through prayer, we are saying we know God can make good things out of what doesn't make sense.

Instead of worrying about how to do something or wondering if it will turn out okay, we pray!

Paul was great at reminding Christians to pray. He talked about prayer a lot. He may have understood a lot about prayer because there's not much else you can do when you're in prison, and that's where Paul spent a bunch of time!

During one of the times Paul was in prison, he wrote a letter to the church in Philippi (pronounced FILL-uh-pie). That letter became the book of Philippians (pronounced fill-IP-ee-uhns).

If you read all of Philippians, you will notice that Paul is filled with joy. Why do you think this is? Let's read some of his words:

Don't fret or worry. Instead of worrying, pray. Let petitions and praises shape your worries into prayers, letting God know your concerns. Before you know it, a sense of God's wholeness, everything coming together for good, will come and settle you down.

Philippians 4:6-7

Some of these words might be new to you. Here's what they mean:

- **Fret** means "worry."
- **Petitions** are requests.
- **Concerns** are troubles or worries.
- A **sense** is a feeling.

Paul has a lot to say in these verses. Let's take a closer look.

"Don't fret or worry."

At first these words might sound like Paul is giving a command. Or they might remind you of a dad telling a child to behave—like "Don't do this or you will get in trouble!"

But right before these words, Paul says, "The Lord is coming soon" (Philippians 4:5, NLT). He's saying, "You don't have to worry, because God is coming to be with you." These words are meant to calm the people down and help them feel peace.

"Instead of worrying, pray."

Paul tells the people what they can do instead of worrying. They can pray! Prayer is an action. Worrying keeps us from acting. It's like giving up on a project because we don't think it can ever work.

But praying is like asking for help with the first few pieces of a puzzle or following the first direction in a craft kit. It means believing something good can happen because you trust God to help you.

What is something you're worrying about right now?

What would you like to say to God about this worry today?

"Let petitions and praises shape your worries into prayers, letting God know your concerns."
Once upon a time, a young woman was learning and wondering a lot of things about God. She started writing down her thoughts and sharing them with others. While many people thanked her for what she was sharing, lots of people didn't agree with her thoughts. They sent her really angry letters. Many of them were hurtful and made her very sad.

What do you think she did with those letters?

You may be thinking she threw them away or tore them up. But she didn't! She took those pages of hurtful words and folded them into beautiful shapes. As she folded, she prayed for the people who wrote the letters and for herself.

She took something that could have made her upset and turned it into something else. As she did, she told God her concerns, and it changed her. It changed other people too. Someone even told her they were sorry for the hurtful things they had written to her.[4]

How do you think praying about your worries can change you?

"Before you know it, a sense of God's wholeness, everything coming together for good, will come and settle you down."
This is the moment when you can see that your project is coming together. You started building the craft step by step. You know that you will be able to see the whole thing soon. You know it's going to be good if you keep going!

In all areas of our lives, God is the one who brings wholeness. God can fix the things in our world that broke because of sin. One day, when he comes to gather those who follow him, everything in our world will be whole again.

How does it feel to know that God will fix everything one day?

● ● ● ● ●

There's one other thing to know about praying when we're worried or sad. Sometimes when we are upset, it's hard to talk. Perhaps that has happened to you when you were sick or crying. Maybe someone asked what was wrong but you couldn't tell them what you needed.

God knows this about us. He knows that our prayers may not always match what we really want to say. That's why the Holy Spirit helps us with our prayers. Here's what the Bible says about that:

> If we don't know how or what to pray, it doesn't matter. He does our praying in and for us, making prayer out of our wordless sighs, our aching groans.
> Romans 8:26

Even groans can be prayers. Isn't that amazing? God really does want to hear from us no matter what.

Chapter 20
When Can I pray?

God made us to have lots of feelings. You are feeling a certain way right now. You might have felt a different way earlier. And you might feel another way later!

Take a look at these feeling words. Put your finger on a feeling you are having right now or have had today.

sad	happy	confused	excited	angry	bored
sick	disappointed	thankful	tired	troubled	

Look at the words again. See if there's a feeling you've *never* had. If so, what is it?

Chances are you have had most of these feelings at some point—and probably a few other feelings too! God knows that we will have different feelings at different times. Because he gave us our emotions, we can trust him with our feelings.

Just like there are many right ways to pray, you don't need to have a certain feeling when you pray. You can pray anytime, no matter how you're feeling. People talked to God with lots of different emotions in the Bible:

- Moses told God he didn't feel ready to go help the Israelites escape from Egypt (Exodus 4:10-13).

- David cried out to God when he felt forgotten or when his enemies were winning (Psalm 56:1-4, for example).

- Daniel prayed even though it meant he would be with lions in a pit (Daniel 6:6-10).

- Jesus gave thanks when God the Father provided food and drink (Mark 14:22-24).

One place in the Bible that shows a lot of feelings is the Psalms. The prayers in the Psalms are poetic songs. They give us words to say to God when we are happy or sad or feeling any other way!

Look up the verses on the left. Then see if you can match each verse to the emotion we see in it on the right.

Psalm 9:1	upset
Psalm 31:6	thankful
Psalm 51:1	happy
Psalm 102:1	troubled
Psalm 120:1	sorry for sin

In so many of the psalms, the writers are not afraid to say what they mean. They're not afraid to ask God for what they need. That's because when we know God, we are in a relationship with God. Just like we talk to and listen to other people we love, we talk to and listen to God through prayer. It's a conversation. A **conversation** involves talking *and* listening.

But talking with God is also more than just talking with a friend. He is our King and Savior. He deserves respect and praise.

When you think of a king (or queen), perhaps you picture a crown and a throne room. To speak with royalty, people must follow certain rules. Even the children of royalty sometimes have to follow special rules to see their important parents!

First, if you want to see a king or queen, you must either be invited or ask for permission to come to their throne room. When you see royalty, you have to bow. In some places and times in history, if a person didn't do those things, they might have been put to death for their disrespect.

But even though Jesus is our King, we never have to get permission to come and speak to him. We never have to be afraid of forgetting something like bowing to him. We are free. We can be certain that God wants to hear from us and will listen.

Here are some words from John about when we come to God with our prayers:

> How bold and free we then become in his presence, freely asking according to his will, sure that he's listening. And if we're confident that he's listening, we know that what we've asked for is as good as ours.
> 1 John 5:14-15

Some of these words might be new to you. Here's what they mean:

- **Bold** means "brave" or "fearless."
- **Presence** is being near someone or something.
- **According to his will** means "fitting with God's plan."
- **Confident** means "certain" or "sure."

Read those verses again out loud and notice how excited John is about coming to God and telling God about his needs.

Now do motions with some of the words while you read the verse out loud. Here are some ideas for motions:

- "Free": Throw your arms out like you are winning a race.
- "Presence": Draw invisible circles in the air around where you are standing (or sitting).
- "Listening": Point to your ears.
- "Know": Point to your head.
- "As good as ours": Pretend to receive a gift.

Now that you know that God cares about all our feelings and that we can come to him at any time, ask yourself the following questions.

What is a new thing I've learned about prayer?

How can I make prayer a bigger part of my life?

Then take a moment to picture God on a throne as you read the following words:

Let us come boldly to the throne of our gracious God. There we will receive his mercy, and we will find grace to help us when we need it most.
Hebrews 4:16, NLT

Tell God anything you are thinking right now!

Section 5
Fellowship!

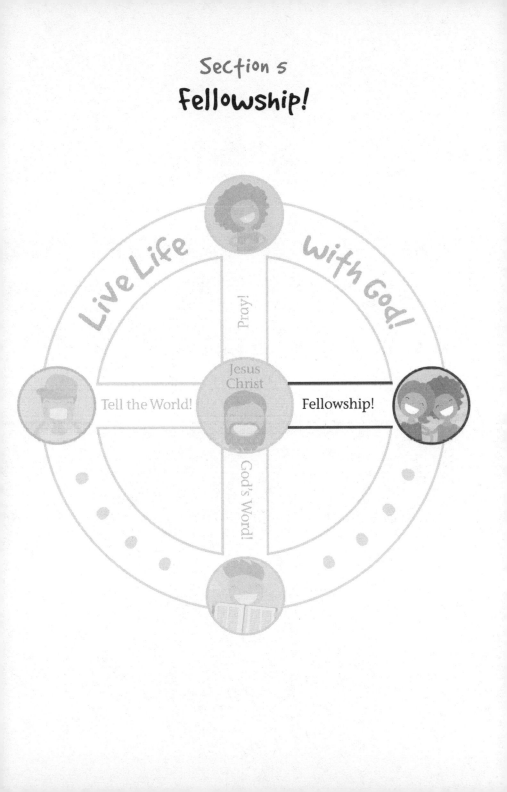

Live Life

With God!

Pray!

Jesus
Christ

Tell the World!

Fellowship!

God's Word!

We saw it, we heard it, and now we're telling you so you can experience it along with us, this experience of communion with the Father and his Son, Jesus Christ.

1 John 1:3

Let's see how inventive we can be in encouraging love and helping out, not avoiding worshiping together as some do but spurring each other on, especially as we see the big Day approaching.

Hebrews 10:24-25

Chapter 21
What is fellowship?

Every day after school Nadia went to the local community center. She loved to be there because of the art studio. Mrs. Mills, the art teacher, always had great ideas and was ready to help Nadia get items out to use.

"Good afternoon, Nadia! How was school today?" Mrs. Mills asked.

"Fine," the girl answered as she hung her backpack on a hook. "I passed my spelling test. But I'm more excited about making something here today."

"What's your plan? What do you want to create?"

"I want to make a vase for my best friend, Collette! Her birthday is next Saturday," Nadia said.

"Okay, then," said Mrs. Mills.

Nadia glanced around the room as Mrs. Mills prepared the clay. Nadia enjoyed being part of a group of people who loved art as much as she did.

Because Nadia was still new to ceramics projects, Mrs. Mills threw the clay onto the wheel for Nadia. The girl could tell the woman was an expert because the chunk landed in just the right spot on the wheel.

Nadia turned the wheel on. Mrs. Mills reminded her to be gentle as she moved her hands up and down the clay. Once Nadia placed her two thumbs in the middle, the clay moved upward and began to form a vase.

She messed up a couple of times, but that didn't matter. She had seen plenty of other students at the center make mistakes and begin again. Sometimes the other kids would make something beautiful out of the mess instead.

Once Nadia was happy about the way her vase looked, she asked Mrs. Mills to remove it from the wheel.

"Your vase will be drying for a couple of days, and then we will fire it in the kiln. What color do you want to glaze it after that?" the teacher inquired.

"Pink! That's Collette's favorite color!" Nadia replied with a grin.

"Pink it is! I will make sure I have pink glaze for you," Mrs. Mills assured her.

Throughout the week, the girl made other things to give to her friend. One day she worked with some other girls at a scrap-paper table to make Collette a card. The next day Nadia created a ribbon tie to put around the vase and showed a younger child who was new to the center how to make one too.

On the day she got to glaze the vase, her friend Jacob was also glazing something. They talked about how their week was going.

Normally, at home or school, Nadia preferred to be alone. But she felt differently when she was with others in the art room. She wanted to be in that big, messy room with these people. She learned from Mrs. Mills and was also able to teach those around her.

On the day of Collette's birthday, Nadia was so excited to place the card and vase with some daisies on her friend's porch. She rang the doorbell and hid behind a bush. Nadia knew Collette would answer the door because she had called Collette's mom and told her about the surprise.

"Oh look!" Collette shrieked. "All my favorites! Who did this?"

Nadia came out from behind the bush. "Me!" she announced.

The two friends hugged.

Collette opened her card. "How did you make this? It's so pretty."

"I made it at the community center art room."

"I want to come sometime. I'd like to learn how to do this too," Collette stated.

"Of course! I will show you where everything is in the art room. You can meet my friends there. We would love to have you." Nadia hugged her friend again before they carried the flowers inside.

Why did Nadia love going to the community center?

What did Nadia like about being in the art room?

Why did Collette want to go to the community center too?

● ● ● ● ●

Isn't it wonderful to have a place where you feel you belong? People at the community center knew Nadia by name and what she had faced at school that day. Even though the children and Mrs. Mills were all very different people with different ages and different talents and abilities, they all loved art. The thing they loved brought them together and made them feel like they belonged.

And that excitement was for more than just the people in their group! Even Collette wanted to join in the fun!

That's what can happen when we are with other Christians. A word Christians often use for spending time with one another is **fellowship**.

Fellowship is part of having faith, because God never meant for us to live alone. When others see our love for God and for being together, it's possible they will want to join in with us.

Chapter 22
What's good about fellowship?

Let's read this verse together:

> We saw it, we heard it, and now we're telling you so you can experience it along with us, this experience of communion with the Father and his Son, Jesus Christ.
> 1 John 1:3

Some of these words might be new to you. Here's what they mean:

- **Experience** is knowing something by doing or seeing it.
- **Communion** is having a close relationship with someone.

Read 1 John 1:1-4. By now, I bet you can guess who wrote the verses you just read. That's right—it's the disciple John! When he says "we" in these verses, he means the disciples who knew Jesus and followed Jesus when he was on earth.

What did the disciples see and hear when they were with Jesus?

In what ways did they share their experience with others?

Right after Jesus went back to heaven, the Holy Spirit came to help Jesus' followers. That same day Peter (another disciple) shared the Good News about Jesus with a crowd of people. Three thousand people chose to trust and obey Jesus that day.

The **believers**—those who followed Jesus—began to live their lives together. They needed each other for many reasons.

Check out these next verses. In the space below the passage, make a list of the things the believers did together.

All the believers were together. They shared everything they had. They sold property and other things they owned. They gave to anyone who needed something. Every day they met together in the temple courtyard. They ate meals together in their homes. Their hearts were glad and sincere. They praised God. They were respected by all the people. Every day the Lord added to their group those who were being saved.
Acts 2:44-47, NIrV

This group of people also formed the first church. The church is not just a building—it's the people of God! The church is like a family. Sometimes the church is even called the family of God.

What do people in a family do for one another?

How does your family work together? Or how have you seen families work together?

Paul also said the church is like a body. Maybe you've heard someone call the church the **body of Christ**. That means each person has something different to do. It's like how your ears, elbows, and knees each do something different and important. Together, as the body of Christ, we can keep moving and working in the world (Romans 12:4-5).

Guess who is the "head" of the body of Christ? If you said Jesus, you are right! God the Father put Jesus in charge of everything. That includes the church. Here are some words from Paul about this very thing:

The church is Christ's body, in which he speaks and acts, by which he fills everything with his presence.
Ephesians 1:23

The word "presence" isn't about the gifts you get for your birthday. (That word is spelled "p-r-e-s-e-n-t-s.") Remember from chapter 20—**presence** is being near to someone. The church is the presence of God here on earth.

When we come together (and also go out to other places), we are showing others what God is like. We are able to show Jesus to the world by the way we treat others, encourage others, and provide for others. God created us to love him and love others. Jesus said that loving him is the greatest command. Loving others is like the other greatest command (Mark 12:30-31). Our love for one another and for everyone else around us is how we show God's presence to the world.

God never meant for humans to be alone. He created us with relationship in mind (Genesis 2:18). Through fellowship with those who also follow Jesus, we have the "experience of communion with the Father and his Son, Jesus Christ" like John wrote about in his letter (1 John 1:3). Jesus said it best:

"When two or three of you are together because of me, you can be sure that I'll be there."
Matthew 18:20

Chapter 23

Who do I fellowship with?

You may be wondering who to fellowship with. Good question! He wants us to spend time with other believers. When you go to church, it can feel easiest to be around people who have a lot in common with you. Sometimes you might meet people at church who are harder to be friends with. But remember, everyone who follows Jesus is part of the body of Christ. God wants us to treat other people with kindness and forgiveness (Ephesians 4:32). We can show love to and pray for difficult people too.

What about when you are not at church? No matter where you go, it's a good idea to think about who you hang out with a lot. We need to choose our close friends carefully because friendship is a part of fellowship too.

The Bible gives us some ideas on choosing friends. In fact, the book of Proverbs has some verses about this very thing. Proverbs is all about wisdom. **Wisdom** is knowing how to make good and right choices.

Let's find the book of Proverbs in your Bible. (Hint: Proverbs is right after the book of Psalms. Open your Bible to the middle and keep going a little more.)

Now look up the following verses. See if you can match what you read with the correct message on the right.

Proverbs 28:7	A good friend helps you be better, like when steel sharpens steel.
Proverbs 13:20	Friends who follow God give good advice.
Proverbs 27:17	Spending time with foolish friends leads to trouble.

The verses are a little like a math problem and could be written this way:

- wise friends = helpers in making good choices and following God
- foolish friends = helpers in making bad choices and getting in trouble

So how do we know what a good and wise friend is like? Let's read these verses together. See if you can fill in the blanks with the right words in the box.

Proverbs 17:17 A good friend is _____ and sticks close to you like a brother.

Proverbs 27:6 A good friend says words you can _____ and won't lie to you.

Proverbs 27:9 The sweetness of a friend comes from their honest _____ (NIrV).

trust	loyal	advice

When you are around friends who trust and obey God like you do, you can help each other move forward in knowing Jesus. You can learn from each other and tell each other what Jesus is doing for you.

In this book, we've looked at a lot of verses in the Old Testament written by a man named David. He went from being a young shepherd to being king of Israel years later.

Early in his life, David made a friend named Jonathan. Jonathan was the son of King Saul. At first King Saul liked David, but then he changed his mind. David became famous, and Saul became jealous.

David and Jonathan had already become friends by this point.

Jonathan knew that even though he was the son of King Saul, God had chosen David to become the next king. He trusted God's plan for his friend.

Acting differently from his father, Jonathan was never jealous of David. The Bible says that Jonathan was David's "number-one advocate and friend" (see 1 Samuel 18:1-4). Saul became so jealous of David that he tried to kill him. Jonathan warned David that he was in danger (1 Samuel 19:1-3). Jonathan and David also made a promise to care for one another's families (1 Samuel 20:11-17). After Jonathan died, David did what he had promised (2 Samuel 9:1).

We looked at Proverbs 17:17 earlier. One version says, "A friend is always loyal, and a brother is born to help in time of need" (NLT).

In what ways does this verse remind you of David and Jonathan's friendship?

Now think about your life·

Who are your closest friends right now?

Who is someone you think could be a good friend? How can you be a good friend to that person?

How can you and your friends help each other trust Jesus more?

You probably had some good answers to that last question. Here are some other ideas, in case you need more:

- Talk about what's going on in your life (Galatians 6:2).
- Share Bible verses with each other (Ephesians 5:19; Colossians 3:16).
- Pray for each other (James 5:16).
- Give thanks for each other (Philippians 1:3).

One last thing to think about when it comes to friendships is talking to someone who is older than you are. Parents and other adults who know God can give you good ideas on who to fellowship with and how to choose someone who will be a good friend.

It's okay if some of your friends aren't Christians yet. In fact, you can be the one to tell them about Jesus! We will talk more about that in the next section of this book.

Chapter 24
What do we do when we fellowship?

Let's read these verses together:

> Let's see how inventive we can be in encouraging love and helping out, not avoiding worshiping together as some do but spurring each other on, especially as we see the big Day approaching.
> Hebrews 10:24-25

Some of these words might be new to you. Here's what they mean:

- **Inventive** means "creative."
- **Encouraging** is helping someone keep going.
- **Avoiding** is staying away from something.
- **Spurring on** means "encouraging."
- **The big Day** is when Jesus will come back for those who trust and obey him.

Read Hebrews 10:19-25.

Have you ever been to a major sports event or seen one on television?

What did you see during the game? You might have noticed the players on the field, the coaches on the sidelines, or the fans in the stands.

Sometimes watching the fans is just as fun as watching the players. Some fans get pretty crazy and creative. They wear bright T-shirts, paint their faces, hold silly signs, and shake noisemakers.

Even if fans sitting together don't know each other, it's likely they will all get excited together. They might talk about the amazing plays that happen or jump up and down together. It's like the fans become instant friends because they have something in common—they're cheering for the same team.

The first part of Hebrews 10:24-25 urges us to be inventive, or creative, as we meet with other believers. That doesn't mean we have to get loud or paint our faces! But it does mean we greet each other with excitement, encourage each other, and help each other.

We are filled with joy when we are together because we are all part of something bigger. We are part of God's family.

What is the most creative thing you've ever seen christians do together?

How can you encourage or help someone this week?

Let's look at the next part of Hebrews 10:24-25: "not avoiding worshiping together as some do."

Sometimes people wonder if it's okay to follow God on their own without attending a church. They may wonder if they *have to* fellowship with other people who have faith in God.

While it's good to have our own time with God, he has made it clear that we shouldn't stay away from other Christians all the time. We need each other!

Part of fellowship is finding others who can relate to you or keep you going when you want to give up. That's what "spurring each other on" is (Hebrews 10:25).

It's cheering someone on by saying, "You can do this! You've got this!" It's reminding people of God's promises in the Bible. It's sitting with someone who is sad and telling them, "I'm sorry that hard thing happened to you."

There is also a very important clue about what we do when we fellowship. See if you can figure out what that word is based on the first and last letters. (Hint: You can look at Hebrews 10:24-25 again.)

W __ __ __ __ __ P^s

When we come together, we come to worship God. In worship, we remember that Jesus is at the center of our lives and our relationships with others.

Worshiping together can be done in many different ways at different times. One common way to worship as God's family is by meeting with other believers once a week in a building or another regular location. Some churches call this a **worship service**.

Churches who follow Jesus share some similar things. For example, church buildings often have at least one cross, either outside or inside. That symbol is to remind us that Jesus fixed the relationship between us and God when he died on the cross. The cross makes Jesus the center of all that God's family does together.

God's Word is an important part of the weekly gathering. While we can read Scripture on our own, local churches are where we can learn even more about what God has to say to us. Pastors and other leaders tell us more about what a life of loving and following Jesus looks like.

Also, at weekly gatherings, there is usually music. Even if there are no instruments, there will probably be singing. Joining together in music is another way we worship God as his family.

Finally, the last part of Hebrews 10:24-25 reminds us that we will fellowship with other Christians forever. An English minister named Charles Spurgeon, who lived and preached in the nineteenth century, once spoke in a sermon about singing praises to God. I'm paraphrasing, but he talked about how praise is where we practice the songs we will sing to God forever and ever. We learn to sing now.

Then we will keep singing together after Jesus comes to bring all believers into heaven.[6]

The Bible gives us a beautiful glimpse of what it will be like when all believers from everywhere on earth are joined in singing praise to God. Read Revelation 7:9-12. Revelation is the last book of the Bible, which means that God shows us from the beginning of the Bible to the end that we need fellowship!

After you read these verses, close your eyes. Imagine this scene, and think about what it will look like when all Christians are praising God together. Then, the next time you are singing with other followers of Jesus, remember that this is practice for when we will all be with Jesus forever!

Chapter 25
How can I be involved in fellowship?

Five-year-old Hannah took her position at the piano. She plunked out the tune to "Amazing Grace." The room was silent except for the notes coming from the piano.

Hannah wasn't any more talented than anyone else her age, but the people around her listened closely because they were so grateful that she was playing music for them.

When Hannah was done, she walked quickly back to her seat. The people in the room clapped quietly, and her parents gave her a hug.

Even though Hannah was only five years old, she was participating in fellowship. There's a good chance Hannah will continue to find new and creative ways to encourage people around her for the rest of her life. That's because her church understands she's part of God's family, no matter what age she is.

The same thing is true about you!

You might be young, but you have so much to offer as you fellowship. First Timothy 4:12 says, "Don't let anyone put you down because you're young. Teach believers with your life: by word, by demeanor, by love, by faith, by integrity."

Paul wrote these words to a man named Timothy. (Remember

Timothy from chapter 12?) Paul taught Timothy how to lead in the church. Timothy was young when he became a leader. Paul wanted him and other people in the church to know that even though they were young, they were just as capable of teaching others.

One way you can teach others is by the way you choose to live—by loving others, by trusting and obeying God, and by speaking kind and wise words. Remember, **encouragement** is telling others they can keep going because God will help them.

Take a minute to think about how you can be part of your church. Here are some ideas:

- drawing
- painting
- playing instruments
- singing
- dancing

- writing letters or cards
- reading aloud
- speaking helpful words
- including others in activities

After looking at the list, answer these questions:

What do you think about these ideas?

What are some other ideas you have?

What is your favorite talent? What is one way you can use that talent for fellowship in your church?

It's a good idea to talk with a parent or other adult who knows your church well. Some churches might have rules about what you can do during fellowship times. But the adults you talk to also might have some other good ideas to help you decide.

Remember how Paul taught Timothy how to lead in the church? Paul showed people how to lead both by talking to them in person and by writing letters.

Even though Paul was far away from these people who were part of God's church, he kept remembering them and praying for them. He sent them kind and encouraging words. This is fellowship too.

Here is a part of one of Paul's letters:

I, Paul, am writing this letter. Silas and Timothy join me in writing.

We are sending this letter to you, the members of the church in Thessalonica. You belong to God the Father and the Lord Jesus Christ.

May grace and peace be given to you.

We always thank God for all of you. We keep on praying for you. We remember you when we pray to our God and Father. Your work is produced by your faith. Your service is the result of your love. Your strength to continue comes from your hope in our Lord Jesus Christ.

Brothers and sisters, you are loved by God. We know that he has chosen you.

1 Thessalonians 1:1-4, NIrV

Who helped Paul write this letter?

Who was the letter written to?

What did Paul do for this church?

What helpful things did Paul say to this church? (There are lots, so it's okay if you don't find them all.)

Would you want to receive a letter like this? Why or why not?

Receiving a letter is fun. It's wonderful to know that someone far away thought of you and sent you a message. Did you know that there are churches all over the world right now who need to hear from other believers? You can fellowship with these people too.

Some of these churches don't have much money. Others live in unsafe places where not many people around them like to hear about Jesus.

These people need prayer. You can pray for them. In some cases, you can fellowship by writing them letters or cards. It's possible that your local church has relationships with other churches around the world. Ask an adult who goes to church with you how you can fellowship with these people who are part of the church in different places.

No matter what, remember that *you* are part of the church! See how creative you can be in your fellowship. There are so many possibilities, and God will help you encourage others in his family.

Tell the World!

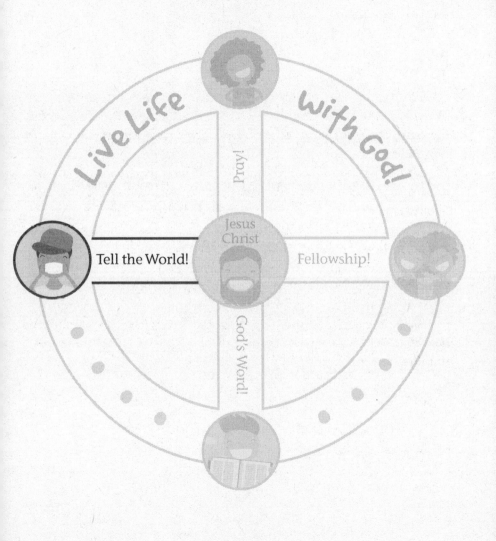

Jesus said to them, "Come with me. I'll make a new kind of fisherman out of you. I'll show you how to catch men and women instead of perch and bass."

Matthew 4:19

It's news I'm most proud to proclaim, this extraordinary Message of God's powerful plan to rescue everyone who trusts him, starting with Jews and then right on to everyone else!

Romans 1:16

Chapter 26
What is witnessing?

Hunter couldn't wait until the weekend. He was ready to go fast during the kids' fun run on Saturday. He had been practicing a lot!

The fun run wasn't the only great thing happening. Hunter's grandpa liked to run too. Grandpa Dean had competed in all kinds of races, even in different states. This would be the first time Hunter and his grandfather would get to run together. The plan was for Grandpa Dean to run with Hunter until the kids' run was over. Then he would keep going in the longer race.

Earlier that week, Grandpa Dean had shown up with a gift for Hunter: a new water bottle. Hunter felt like a real runner.

The day before the race, Hunter's teacher, Mr. Keith, asked if the class had anything to share about the upcoming weekend. The boy's hand shot up in the air.

"Yes, Hunter?"

"I get to run in a race this weekend with my grandpa. I can't wait!" Hunter informed his teacher.

"Well, that's wonderful!" Mr. Keith replied. "Is this the race they are setting up for downtown?"

"Yes, that's the one," Hunter answered with a large smile.

"I hope you have fun! I bet it will be great," encouraged Mr. Keith.

At recess, Hunter decided to run around the edge of the playground. He asked if any friends wanted to come too. Emma and Will joined him.

"Are you really running in a race tomorrow?" Emma asked.

"Yep," Hunter said. He slowed down a moment for Will to catch up.

"What makes you want to do something like that?" Will panted. "This is hard."

"Have you ever been to a race?"

"Well, no. What's so great about it?" Will grabbed the side of his stomach.

"Cramp?" Emma asked. "We'll slow down."

Even though Hunter was kind of sad to not be running fast anymore, he was excited to tell Will more about races.

"At a race, there is something for everyone, even if you aren't running," Hunter said.

Emma jumped in. "They give out ribbons and other prizes, too, right?"

"Yes. And, of course, runners need people cheering for them. It's hard not to give up, especially on hills." Hunter let out a small groan as he thought about the hill he would have to run up the next day.

"That makes sense," Will said. "I can't wait to hear how it goes for you."

Just then the bell rang and recess ended. The students lined up outside their classroom.

Early the next morning, Hunter's dad woke him up. Hunter suddenly remembered that it was race day. He rushed to find Grandpa Dean. They grabbed their water bottles and were on their way.

At the race, Grandpa Dean attached their runner's numbers to the front of their shirts. Hunter's dad promised to be at the finish line for the fun run. Then he and Hunter would go get ready to cheer for Grandpa Dean at the finish line across town.

After some stretching, everyone lined up. A loud bang went off, and Hunter was running toward the finish line! He knew his grandpa could keep up, so he just went as fast as he could.

It felt so good to get to the finish line and receive a ribbon. Hunter's dad hugged him as they waved goodbye to Grandpa Dean.

"See you soon!" Hunter shouted.

Hunter loved hearing the crowds cheer as he and his dad went across the town. They got to the finish line a few minutes before Grandpa Dean crossed. Hunter even saw Will across the road and waved. His friend smiled and held up a colorful sign that said "Go! Go! Go!"

Just then a news crew approached Hunter and his dad to see if they would like to be interviewed. Hunter thought, *I'm going to be famous!*

"Why did you choose to be a part of today's race?" the newswoman asked, putting a microphone in front of Hunter's dad.

"It's a great time for family to be together," he answered. "We were able to witness people running, laughing, and cheering for each other."

"How about you, young man?" The microphone came toward Hunter's face.

"I was excited to run with my grandpa!" Hunter said with a big grin.

The newswoman turned to the camera and said, "You heard it here, folks. It's family first at this race, no matter when you finish."

● ● ● ● ●

Have you ever heard the word "witness"? A **witness** is someone who saw an event happen. When someone tells others about what happened, it is called **witnessing**.

Perhaps "witnessing" is a word you've heard at your church or around other people who follow Jesus. That's because God has given Christians the job of telling others about him and the life he offers.

Let's think back to the story about Hunter.

Who did Hunter tell about the race?

In what ways was Hunter a witness?

Who else was a witness in the story?

In the next part of this book, we'll discover more about what it's like to witness—to tell the world about God.

Chapter 27
Why do we witness?

Let's read this verse together:

> Jesus said to them, "Come with me. I'll make a new kind of fisherman out of you. I'll show you how to catch men and women instead of perch and bass."
> Matthew 4:19

Some of these words might be new to you. Here's what they mean:

> • **perch and bass:** kinds of fish

Matthew is the first book in the New Testament. You might remember that it's one of the four Gospels, which tell us about the life of Jesus.

The writer, Matthew, was one of Jesus' disciples. He was a tax collector. During New Testament times, people didn't like tax collectors because some of them cheated and stole money. Jesus called Matthew to leave his job of collecting money and learn from Jesus instead.

Now read Matthew 4:18-22. (You can probably look this up yourself by using the Table of Contents in your Bible. If not, ask an adult for help.)

How would you feel if a stranger walked up to you and said, "Come with me"? You'd probably be a little confused or worried, right?

So then why did these men just drop their things to follow Jesus?[7]

Well, Jesus was a rabbi. A **rabbi** is a teacher. Rabbis chose their students, who were called **disciples**. It was an honor to be chosen as a disciple.

If you weren't chosen to learn from a rabbi, then you just went and worked a regular job. That's what these men were doing. They were working as fishermen.

Now imagine you are one of these fishermen. Perhaps some of your friends were chosen to be disciples by other rabbis but you weren't. Then along comes a rabbi and he says, "Drop your nets and come with me."

That's pretty exciting. It's like Jesus was saying, "I'm choosing you! I want you to be with me and learn from me."

And this was only the beginning. In this book we've already heard from some of the disciples who followed Jesus that day. Can you name one or two of them? (Hint: Their names are in the verses you just read!)

Choosing to trust and obey Jesus was a first step for these young men, just like your decision to trust and obey Jesus is your first step to living life with God. But that's not where we stop.

Still thinking about the verses from Matthew 4, answer these questions:

What two things did Jesus promise to teach his new disciples?

What do you think Jesus meant by these promises?

By now you've probably discovered that Jesus didn't really mean the disciples would catch people like they did fish (using nets). Jesus meant that he would show his followers how to follow his ways and *also* how to invite others to know Jesus and follow his ways too.

Throughout the Gospels, Jesus continued to teach the disciples and to call others to trust him always. Jesus changed their lives. None of them were the same after meeting Jesus.

That's because Jesus can change people's lives in every way.

What are some ways Jesus has changed your life?

Thinking about how Jesus has changed you is one way to begin telling others about Jesus.

Remember, each of us has an "old life," where we do the opposite of what God wants us to do. Those wrong things are sin, and sin brings death.

The "new life" is the new way to live when we accept Jesus. It's all the opposites of sin.

Many people don't know about eternal life. They don't know that their lives can be better because of Jesus. They don't know he offers them the ability to know him and talk with him and read his Word.

Take a few minutes to go back and look at chapter 2 in this book. This is where you began on your journey on the obedient life with Jesus at the center. When someone hears about Jesus for the first time, this is where they will begin.

They will need to find out how great Jesus is! They will need to discover he's in charge of everything. They will need to learn that Jesus cares about every part of their life and that he has promised to always be with those who trust him.

How can others find these things out about Jesus? You can be the one to tell them!

Chapter 28
Who Can I witness to?

In the Bible God talks about offering people salvation. **Salvation** is being saved. We also mentioned earlier in this book that Jesus is our **Savior** because he saved us from sin. "Salvation" and "Savior" sound similar because both words are about being saved or rescued.

Early in the Bible, God gave salvation to the Israelites (later called Jews). Do you remember how he rescued the Israelites from slavery in Egypt? All through the Bible, God kept saving his people.

Have you ever heard the stories of the wall around a city named Jericho coming down (Joshua 6:1-20)? Or maybe you have heard the story of a young man named David defeating the giant named Goliath (1 Samuel 17:32-50). Those are just a couple of times when God helped his people win battles and stay safe. He saved them!

Sometimes God's people made bad choices, and they needed to be forgiven for their sins. God was always ready to save them from that, too:

"I've wiped the slate of all your wrongdoings.
    There's nothing left of your sins.
Come back to me, come back.
    I've redeemed you."
Isaiah 44:22

God also offered salvation from sin to people in other countries. An example of that can be seen in the book of Jonah. God was willing to save the people of Nineveh from their wicked ways. Jonah ran away because he didn't think the people of Nineveh deserved to be saved. He didn't want to tell them that God was willing to rescue them from their sins.

In John 3:16, we find out that God loved the whole world, so he sent Jesus, his only Son, to die for humanity's sins. Anyone who believes in him—not just the Israelites—will be saved. Second Corinthians 5:15 tells us that Jesus "died for everyone" (NLT).

A lot of the teaching Jesus did was to the Jews (the great-great-great-great-great-grandchildren of Israelites like Moses and David and Solomon in the Old Testament). His disciples were all Jews. When Jesus talked about being the Good Shepherd, he also said there were other sheep (people he loved) who had not yet been brought into his care (John 10:16). But they would be in the future.

That is because God made it possible for the whole world to be saved. First he went to the Jews, the ones he had made his people in the Old Testament, but salvation was for people called Gentiles, too. **Gentiles** are not Jews—they are all the other people in the world.

After Jesus died and rose again, he came to his disciples. Jesus gave them a great command so they would know who to tell about God's salvation:

"Go and make disciples of all the nations. . . . Teach these new disciples to obey all the commands I have given you. And be sure of this: I am with you always, even to the end of the age."
Matthew 28:19-20, NLT

Here are the commands Jesus gave in this passage and what they mean:

- "Go": God intended for everyone to know about him. That means people who trust and obey Jesus don't just stay in one place. If we follow Jesus, sometimes we need to move or look outside the normal places we go each day to find people who don't know him.

- "Make disciples of all the nations": A disciple is a follower, right? God's plan involves the followers of Jesus going and making new followers. Where? All nations. All kinds of people. All over the world.

- "Teach these new disciples to obey": As people hear about Jesus, they will learn to follow him, to pray, to read his Word, to gather with other believers, and to tell others about him. When they do these things, they are living out the obedience in action that is the outer part of the Wheel.

Just before he went back to heaven, Jesus also told his followers to wait in the main city called Jerusalem. **Jerusalem** was where Jews gathered to worship God together in God's Temple. God's Temple was built to be a home for God's presence and power.

Jesus said to stay in Jerusalem until God the Father sent the Holy Spirit to give the disciples power. God's followers would need this power to go out and tell others about Jesus.

Let's look at Jesus' last words before he went back up to heaven:

"When the Holy Spirit comes on you, you will be able to be my witnesses in Jerusalem, all over Judea and Samaria, even to the ends of the world."
Acts 1:8

You may not have heard of these places because they were in a different part of the world. But you already know that Jerusalem was where the disciples were. Judea and Samaria were nearby areas. And, of course, "the ends of the world" meant the same thing it means today. Here Jesus is talking about going as far as you can go to tell others about Jesus.

It's like Jesus is saying, "Start in your hometown. Then go to the nearby cities in your area. Then tell everyone all over the world!"

Not everyone is able to travel around the world. But Jesus wants us all to know we have the special job of telling others about him. You can start right where you are!

What person in your life doesn't know about Jesus yet?

What is one thing about Jesus you would like to tell them?

What other things can you do for this person to show them God's love?

If anything about witnessing feels scary or confusing, you can remember that you have the same power the disciples were given so they could spread the Good News about Jesus. Where is that power from? The Holy Spirit! Take a moment to go back and look at the words in Acts 1:8. Put your finger on the words "you will be able to" and ask the Holy Spirit to give you the power you need at the right time.

Chapter 29
How do we witness?

Let's read this verse together:

It's news I'm most proud to proclaim, this extraordinary Message of God's powerful plan to rescue everyone who trusts him, starting with Jews and then right on to everyone else!
Romans 1:16

Some of these words might be new to you. Here's what they mean:

- **proclaim:** to tell
- **extraordinary:** special; more than ordinary
- **rescue:** to save
- **Jews:** God's special people

We've already read from the book of Romans, like when we talked about how to obey Jesus in chapter 9. Romans was a letter written by Paul after Jesus went back into heaven.

By this time the Holy Spirit had come and helped the disciples share about Jesus outside of Jerusalem. The book of Romans was written to believers of Jesus in Rome. Rome was in a whole other country. The fact that there was a church in Rome means that God's people had obeyed him and gone out to share that Jesus could save all people from their sins.

Read Romans 1:14-17.

Some versions of the Bible use the word "gospel" in verses 15 and 16. **Gospel** means "good news."

From the Author

My children often ask me why I watch the news on television or read about it on the Internet. They feel like the news can be sad or scary. And lots of times it is.

But news can also be about good things. It's also news when we hear about a new baby being born or someone getting married. It can be fun to tell someone good news. One time my husband and I got to tell our children we were taking them to Disneyland.

Our family had just been through a hard time, so this was amazing news to them. It was wonderful to see their smiles, watch them jump up and down, and hear them yell, "Yay!"

Paul was excited to share news with other people—all people. The news he shared is not something that will be fun once. It will change people's lives because it's about Jesus! It had already changed Paul's life.

Who shared the Good News about Jesus with you first?

Have you ever shared the Good News about Jesus with someone else? If so, what happened?

If you haven't had a chance to share the gospel with someone else yet, that's okay. We're going to keep talking about how to do that.

There's another word that people use when talking about the gospel. That word is "evangelism." **Evangelism** is sharing the gospel.

There are many ways to share the gospel with people. You can write about it. You can talk about it. You can even sing about it.

Over the years, people have gotten creative in how they share that Jesus died and rose again. Some people have written and performed plays in churches or in front of other crowds. Others simply stand in busy places and preach from the Bible. Some people use small booklets called **tracts** that help people learn how to become Christians.

One other way you can share about Jesus is by the way you live. When you are following Jesus and living in the ways we've been learning about with the Wheel, others can see that you have something special in your life.

What are some creative ways you can think of to share about Jesus?

At this point, you might be wondering what you should say to someone if they ask about Jesus or want to know more about him. There are no special words you have to say. There isn't one right way to share the gospel.

But here are some ideas about the way it could go. (You already thought about some of this in chapter 27.)

- Tell them the story of your faith, about how you chose to trust and obey Jesus.

- Share what's so great about Jesus.

- Be sure to mention that everyone has sinned—that the things we've done wrong keep us away from the God who loves us and keep us stuck in a broken life. Jesus is the only one who can save us from that old life.

- To move to the new life Jesus offers, a person needs to confess their sins (Psalm 86:5; 1 John 1:9) and then tell Jesus they want to trust and obey him always.

If the person doesn't know what to say to Jesus, there's a prayer they could use in the "How to Become a Christian" section in the back of this book on pages 133–135.

In the last chapter of this section, we'll talk about what happens when we share the gospel. Jesus taught his disciples how to witness, and we can learn from the disciples' example.

Chapter 30
What happens when I witness?

People become Christians in all sorts of different ways. God works through the people around each of us and through the problems that show us we need him.

We've talked about how Peter preached to thousands of people who became Christians in one day (Acts 2:14-41). Peter told them the whole story about God's plan to rescue us from sin by sending Jesus to die and rise again.

There are even more stories to tell from the book of Acts. That's because the disciples were obeying Jesus' command to make new followers. Let's look at a few times when God worked through his people to save others.

An Ethiopian
Philip was a leader in the church at Jerusalem (Acts 6:5-7). Read Acts 8:26-35 to discover an amazing story of Philip witnessing to a man from Ethiopia.

How did Philip know what to do?

What did Philip help the Ethiopian understand?

At the end of the chapter, it says that the Ethiopian "went on down the road as happy as he could be" (Acts 8:39). He heard the truth about Jesus and was so happy. Ethiopia is a country in Africa. It's very possible that the man who talked with Philip went to his home country to tell others about becoming a Christian. (Believe it or not, people have been worshiping Jesus in Ethiopia longer than in most other places in the world!)[8]

This is what often happens after someone is saved. That person wants to tell others the Good News and the story of how Jesus changed their life. Then the gospel spreads, and more and more people want to follow Jesus—all over the world!

Cornelius the Captain

A man named Cornelius was in charge of a group of Roman soldiers. The Romans ruled the land in the time of the New Testament. Romans were not Jews, so the Romans and Jews did not do much together. They ate different foods and had other different ways they lived.

When God told Cornelius (a Roman) to find Peter (a Jew), it might have seemed strange (Acts 10:1 8). Then God told Peter it was okay to go to Cornelius's house (Acts 10:9-23). Peter explained why he had come.

Read Acts 10:34-44.

What are some of the good things Peter shared about Jesus?

What happened while Peter was speaking?

Everyone in Cornelius's house decided to follow Jesus! Peter stayed there for a few more days to teach them more about God and his plans. God was showing both Jews and Romans that he wanted everyone in his family!

A Jailer in Philippi

As Paul continued to go to new places, he ended up in a place called Philippi. Another believer named Silas was with him.

In that area they came upon a woman who was controlled by an evil spirit. The evil spirit helped her tell the future, and some people were using her to make money. After Paul set the woman free by telling the evil spirit to leave, those people got upset with Paul and Silas. So Paul and Silas were beaten and thrown into jail.

Read Acts 16:25-34 to find out what happened after that.

What amazing thing happened in the jail?

What did the jailer ask Paul and Silas?

How did the jailer feel after he believed in God?

● ● ● ● ●

In each of the passages you read, God did something special to show his power. Through the Holy Spirit, Philip knew who to talk with, Peter knew it was okay to go to Cornelius, and Paul and Silas were released from jail.

God is working all the time to reach everyone with his love. In the next few days, talk with Christians in your life, like your family members or friends. Ask them about when and how they decided to follow Jesus. Invite them to also tell you about times when they were able to share the Good News of Jesus with other people.

Pay attention to how different the stories are from one another and how God worked in each person's life. He wants everyone to know that he loves them and that they can have a new life in him.

We don't always know what will happen when we witness. But we can trust that God is working to help us. We are simply told to obey him by telling the Good News when he gives us the opportunity. Of course, we hope that the person (or people) we talk to will choose to follow Jesus.

However, we can be sure that it's not just up to us. God is working too.

Sometimes it takes time for a person to choose to follow Jesus. Maybe it took a little bit of time for you, too. Not everyone is ready to believe in Jesus the first time they hear about him. Remember, it's not all up to you to help them understand. You just get to share about what Jesus has done in your life and how important he is to you. Then you can trust that the Holy Spirit is doing the rest.

Who can you share the gospel with this week?

Spend a few moments praying for that person (or those people) right now. Let God know you trust him to work through you as you witness to other people.

Moving Forward

- -

We have explored so much about life with God, and the exciting thing about living with Jesus is that there are always new things to discover. Here's an important one: You will never be perfect at everything on the Wheel. But keeping Jesus at the center of your life will keep you moving forward.

Remembering that you belong to Jesus will help you know him, always trust him, and obey his commands so you can live the better new life he has for you. Belonging to Jesus means that you are never alone. You always have someone to talk to—because Jesus wants to talk with you at any time! Reading the Bible will keep you hearing from him and knowing his words.

Through fellowship we can be friends with, enjoy, teach, and learn from others who love God too. Witnessing reminds us of God's Good News and helps other people learn about it too so they can be part of God's family. You can be the one to tell them about Jesus!

Let's look one last time at the Wheel.

Place your finger on each part of the Wheel, beginning with Jesus at the center. See if you can recall one thing you discovered in each section of the book.

Next, place your finger on the part of the Wheel that you want to work on this week. Invite another Christian to pray for your life with God. Ask them to remind you over and over that you are loved by him.

In him you live and move each day. You are his (Acts 17:28).

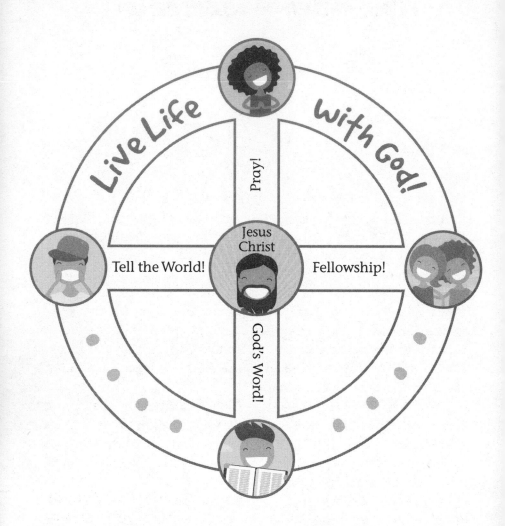

How to Become a Christian

- What does the word "Christian" mean?
- Why do I need to be a Christian?
- How can I become a Christian?

These all are very good questions! Let's check out a couple of verses about this:

Everyone has sinned. No one measures up to God's glory.
Romans 3:23, NIrV

When you sin, the pay you get is death. But God gives you the gift of eternal life. That's because of what Christ Jesus our Lord has done.
Romans 6:23, NIrV

Here's what these verses mean: Everyone sins! Sin separates us from God, and when we are separated from God, death is the result. We all deserve death because we've all chosen to break our relationship with God through sin.

But . . .

God did what we couldn't—he made our broken relationship into something new and whole again. He did this through dying on the cross. Jesus' death paid for all the wrong things we have done and will do. When we choose to believe in Jesus and what he did for us, we are no longer separated from God.

That means death doesn't win! We get eternal life, life forever with God!

Check out the picture below. It helps us understand the verses a little more.

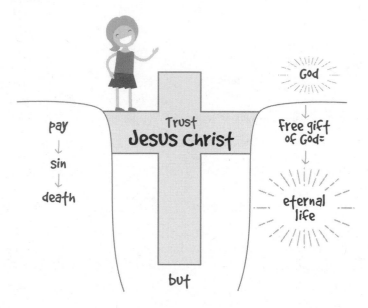

If you believe that the verses you read are true, you can pray this prayer:

Dear God,

I know that I'm a sinner. I need you to forgive me. I believe in Jesus and that he died on the cross and rose again. Now I can be with you forever. Thank you for this gift! I want to trust and obey you every day. In Jesus' name, amen.

If you just prayed this prayer or have ever told God you want to follow him, then you are a Christian!

More Scripture Memory Ideas

Memorizing Scripture is a wonderful way to know Jesus better and remember his better way to live. We've talked about some of the ways to memorize Scripture, but there are so many more! These ideas can be done alone. But it's also fun to do Scripture memory activities with friends and family.

1. Grab a stack of note cards. Write one or two words of the verse you want to memorize on each note card. Mix up the cards and see if you can put the verse in order by laying the cards out on a table or the floor. Do this several times.

2. Look at the most important words in the verse—words like "Jesus" or "listen" or "pray." Say the verse aloud and clap or jump each time you come to one of these words.

3. Write the verse on a whiteboard. Say the verse aloud. Erase one or two words on the board. Say the verse aloud again. Keep erasing words and saying the verse until you have it memorized.

4. Remember those important words in the verse you are learning? This time, write out the verse, but when you come to a main word in the passage, draw a picture instead of writing the word!

Recommended Resources

Topical Memory System for Kids by The Navigators
Topical Memory System for Kids: Be like Jesus! by The Navigators
Seekers: An Interactive Family Adventure in Following Jesus by C. S. Fritz
Spiritual Parenting: An Awakening for Today's Families by Michelle
   Anthony
SeedsFamilyWorship.com

Acknowledgments

First, I want to thank my parents, Rick Ruybalid and Denise Ruybalid Miller, for your love and sacrifice. You had me in church every week and figured out the way to have me in Christian schools for a large part of my life. Those are no small things, and it's because you longed for me to know and love God and his Word. Mission accomplished!

To my brother, David: What can I say? You are one of my best friends, and I trust you to help me unscramble my brain about God and church and Scripture and the latest book I read. I wouldn't know what to do without you. I know not every brother and sister have the relationship we have, and I never want to take our closeness for granted.

To my husband, Jeff: You have always believed in me. I still have the hard copy of the *Writer's Market 2001* you gifted me. I know we have the Internet now and that resource takes up enough shelf space for three paperbacks, but it reminds me of how far we've come—together. I am grateful for your wisdom and how you ask the right questions to find where the real me is buried under all the muck of rules I impose on myself. You're my favorite person to celebrate with when surprises come along—like the opportunity to write this book.

To my children—Kyla, Kaelyn, Keller, and Korbin: It is my great life privilege to be able to disciple you. I long for you to know Jesus and the freedom he gives. He does not give as the world gives, and I hope that I have both taught that to you and modeled it as well. Kyla and Kaelyn—we have been through hard times together as a family in ministry. You inspire me with your bravery, your fierce love for God, and your honest questions. Keller and Korbin—you are at the beginning of your faith journeys. My heart skips a beat to hear you declare, "Jesus loves me" or "God made me." Yes, dear ones. Thank you for reminding me of these truths and for fully being you!

To my grandparents, Ruben and Carol Ruybalid: Thank you for your example of following God and for showing me what it looks like to live for him. You gave me my first tangible experiences in serving others and took great care in gifting me books about faith because you are "book grandparents."

To my dear friends Jessica Williams, Christy Janssen, and Rebekah Largent: You each hold me together in your special ways.

To Jess: I'm convinced God sent us to Kansas for a time so that we could be friends. Your messages crack me up and humble me. You are never afraid to search for what's right. You are the queen of memes and a keeper of my deepest worries and concerns. Thank you for bearing so much with me, even though (too many) miles have kept us apart for a decade now.

To Christy: You encourage me during the ups and downs in ministry and work. You inspire me to work out of my strengths. You shower me with thoughtful gifts, and many of our important conversations happen over food and drink—from cans of Pringles to nights at Bar Louie. Thank you for cheering me on!

To Rebekah: Who could have known when we were kids that we would get to reconnect as both friends and editors? I try to soak in your talents related to editing and writing. I cherish your input on this book. You have a keen eye and offer so much to everyone around you. I am honored to be a recipient of those things.

To Don Pape: I appreciate your energy and excitement over good books! Thank you for shepherding me in my own writing and editing and for the way you are always looking to connect the right people. You approach interactions with an open hand and rejoice when big things arise from simple conversations.

To my editor, Caitlyn: I will never forget the day I got your email titled "An Idea," and what a fun idea it was! We are holding it today. Your presence, thoughts, and desire for God's people to flourish are a blessing to me. Thanks for inviting me deeper into the journey of publishing.

Thank you to my publisher, David Zimmerman, for reaching out with new opportunities, for supporting this book, and for making me a part of the NavPress authors team.

Dr. Greg Carlson, thank you for your guidance and endless encouragement as my adviser at Grace University. You helped me believe that I could do anything for God and his Kingdom and never put limits on what that could be.

Kristin Ritzau, your book and friendship changed my life. Thank you for investing in me and giving me a vision for the freedom we have because of Jesus. I have been able to pass it along in countless ways, including in this book.

Dr. Roger Theimer, thank you for giving me my first paid work writing for children. I still remember the day we launched marshmallows in your office to come up with new activity ideas.

Dearest Jesus, it took me a long time to realize how much you love me and are for me. You have shown me these things through your Word and through your work in my life. I trust you with everything, my Shepherd and King. As Keller likes to say, "Thank you, God, for life."

Glossary of Terms

according to his will: fitting with God's plan

avoiding: staying away from something

believers: Christians—those who follow Jesus

the big Day: when Jesus will come back for those who trust and obey him

body of Christ: the church—the people of God

bold: brave; fearless

Book of The Revelation: God's law

the center: the main or most important thing

Christian: a follower of Christ

commandments: commands

communion: having a close relationship with someone

concerns: troubles; worries

confess: to admit we've done something wrong

confident: certain; sure

conversation: talking and listening to one another

correcting: fixing

disciples: followers; people who follow Jesus

embracing: accepting; welcoming

emerges: appears

encourage: to help someone keep going

encouragement: letting others know they will be okay

evangelism: sharing the gospel

experience: knowing something by doing or seeing it

exposing: showing

extraordinary: special; more than ordinary

faithful: worthy of trust

fellowship: spending time with other people who love God

forever: going on and on without stopping

fret: to worry

genesis: beginning

Gentiles: all the people in the world who aren't Jews

God-breathed: given by God

the gospel: the Good News that God sent his Son, Jesus, to the world to save us by dying on the cross and being raised from the dead so we can be forgiven for our sins

the Gospels: the four books in the Bible about Jesus' life (Matthew, Mark, Luke, and John)

having faith in Jesus: trusting *and* obeying Jesus

the Helper: the Holy Spirit

intercession: praying for other people

inventive: creative

Jerusalem: the city where Jews gathered to worship God together; home of the Temple

Jews: God's special people

keep commandments: to obey

living by faith: listening, trusting, and obeying

meditate on: to think about over and over

memorize: to learn something so well that you can remember it

the Messiah: a title for Jesus

offering: a gift

ordinary: common; regular

paraphrase: a version of the Bible where parts of sentences have been written in a different way to help us understand

perch and bass: kinds of fish

petitions: requests

ponder: to think about

praise: worship; remembering and telling God who he is and the things he has done

prayer: talking to God and listening for him

prayer request: something that someone is asking God for

prayer walk: praying for an area (like a neighborhood, city, or church) where you are walking

presence: being near to someone or something

proclaim: to tell

rabbi: a teacher

rebellion: doing the opposite of what someone in charge wants you to do

request: when you ask for something

rescue: to save

salvation: being saved (in this case, being saved from our sins because of Jesus' death on the cross)

savior: someone who saves or rescues

scribes: people who wrote the Bible onto scrolls by hand

Scripture: God's Word

sense: a feeling

sin: doing the opposite of what God wants us to do; doing wrong

spurring on: encouraging

succeed: to do well

temptation: thinking of doing the wrong thing

tracts: small booklets that tell people how to become Christians

translation: a version of the Bible where each word has been changed from one language into another

united: connected

wisdom: knowing how to make good and right choices

witness: someone who saw an event happen

witnessing: telling others about something that has happened; using our words and lives to let people know that God loves them and wants them to have new life in him

the Word: the Bible; also a name for Jesus

worship service: when Christians gather together to worship God in one place

Notes

1. If you want to find out more about how to become a Christian, check out pages 133–135 in this book.
2. This story is adapted from Luke 15:11-32.
3. These prayer concepts are pulled from *The Prayer Hand*, an illustration by The Navigators.
4. Rachel Held Evans, "What I Learned Turning My Hate Mail into Origami," *Rachel Held Evans* (blog), April 1, 2013, https://rachelheldevans.com /blog/what-i-learned-turning-my-hate-mail-into-origami?rq=origami.
5. The answer is "WORSHIP."
6. The quote can be found in Charles H. Spurgeon, *The Complete Works of C. H. Spurgeon, Volume 36: Sermons 2121 to 2181* (Harrington, DE: Delmarva Publications, 2013), 21. It's in Sermon 2121.
7. For more on how discipleship worked in Jesus' time, see https://www .thattheworldmayknow.com/rabbi-and-talmidim.
8. *Britannica*, "Religion of Ethiopia," accessed August 3, 2022, https://www .britannica.com/place/Ethiopia/Religion.